THE LIFE-FIRST ADVISOR

How the new financial coach connects
'money' with 'meaning'

About the cover
We want to convey that it is a new day for Life-first advisors and the global advice industry. We are looking to the future with optimism and excitement. When our graphic designer Laura Timmermans suggested it, we knew it was perfect!

Published by
Global Adviser Alpha Pty Ltd, Melbourne, Australia ©2017
Right-brain Advisor, Nanaimo, Canada and San Jose California ©2017

Edited by
Lesley Parker, Folio Media, Sydney Australia

Designed by
LT Design - lauratimmermans.ca

ISBN 978-0-9937600-7-5

Our 'Why'

We believe passionately that the approach to advice we advocate can change lives.

This is a new kind of advice. We call it Life-First® because it is a holistic approach based on both the material and non-material needs of people and their families.

We have seen both the benefits of such an approach and the enormous costs of the still too common alternatives in poor advice, product-led advice or no advice at all. Drawing on our two lifetimes of experience, we decided to write this book to encourage other advisors to adopt this way of thinking.

<u>In fact, we believe that it is the only way of the future that clients will pay you for.</u>

We are confident it will improve the lives of your clients, give you enormous pride in your contribution and help you build a sustainable and growing business.

Barry LaValley and David Haintz

Acknowledgments

Barry LaValley

This book is a labor of love for me. I was one of the original participants in a conference of top advisors and leaders in the US in 2002; this was really the first effort to quantify the "life planning approach" to financial planning and was an initiative started by the National Endowment for Financial Education (NEFE). Since that time, the movement has grown and spurred on by such influencers as Mitch Anthony, Carol Anderson and George Kinder. I owe these people my thanks for spurring my own exploration of the topic and the formulation of this "Life-first Approach". In fact, Mitch Anthony wrote the first book on the subject in 2003 called "Your Clients for Life" with the assistance of both Carol Anderson and myself.

Since that time, I have been consistently writing and speaking about how advisors need to take more of a life-planning approach. While I don't feel that advisors are life-planners, I do think that their clients need to be when they develop a long-term plan. In this endeavor, I received support from such people as Marshall Beyer of Moody's Analytics, Leanne Davies of RBC and Carolyn Dabu and Dr. Amy D'Aprix of BMO. I was able to test out my ideas with advisors in both Canada and the US and make sure they were "field tested".

Mark Gochnour of DFA in Austin, Joel Teasdel in Singapore and Nathan Krieger, Caroline Holmes-Hannaford and Brigid Asquith-Hunt with DFA Australia introduced me to the Australian and New Zealand advisor community and allowed me to take my research overseas. Alex Potts and Steve Atkinson of Loring Ward believed in the message and gave me the opportunity to work with Loring Ward advisors to further it. My friend Mark Finke with Cetera in St. Louis was the perfect foil for my ideas and kicked back the ones that didn't fly. He also taught me to speak "American" instead of just "Canadian". Rhonda Latreille of Age Friendly Business helped me understand how aging affects us all and impacts that way that we look at money. Myles Morin has been a mentor and friend and truly understands today's financial advisor and I drew on his knowledge continually over the years.

My wife Melissa stood by me every step of the way and I am forever grateful. She continually pushed me to go further and to believe in myself and I could not have done this without her support and love.

David Haintz

There are many people I would like to thank for helping me become the advisor I was, the advisor to advisors that I am today, and for helping this book become a reality.

To Paul Etheridge, my first mentor over many years, who taught me what clients really needed. To others along the journey that played important and pivotal roles, such as Jim Stackpool, John Bowen, and Bill Bachrach. To the team at MLC ThreeSixty that were instrumental in coaching, mentoring and challenging – such as David Fox, Steve Coyle, Tim Browne and Peter Gommers; all of whom were important in changing my mindset from running a practice, to a business, by working on my business, and not just in it.

To the team at Haintz Financial Services, especially Anne Elliott and Campbell Sorell, who taught me that the only way to attract and retain ideal clients, was to attract and retain the best possible talent to our team; and that it was possible to have a 'family' outside of my own family.

To the Dimensional Fund Advisors Australian and global teams, there are just too many people to thank them all individually. However, I'd like give particular thanks to David Booth, Dave Butler, Glenn Crane, Nigel Stewart, and Nathan Krieger, for their vision, leadership, partnership, friendship, and client centricity.

To the Shadforth staff and partners, especially Tony Fenning, Kevin Bailey, and Tim Rossell, all of whom I respect enormously; for being great friends, mentors, amazing people, and for sharing an incredible journey together.

To Mark Keating and Daniel Isakow for being great friends, confidantes and mentors over many years. To advisers globally for openly, and willingly sharing best practice ideas over the last 28 years; be it in on study tours, site visits, regular study groups, or a skype or phone call.

To my clients for helping me understand what they really needed, and working together to understand and focus on matters more important than money – what the money can help them achieve with their lives.

To Barry LaValley, for being a great friend, and making this labour of love enjoyable.

And finally and most importantly to my family, for being who they are, and for always being there. In particular, a huge thanks to my father Alan, a man of few, but well-chosen words, for encouraging me to join this amazing industry in the first place. And of course, when it comes to 'Life-First', to my family – my wife Michelle and boys Harrison and Jackson for always being there, unconditionally, and helping me to realise and focus on what's more important than money... 'Life-First'.

Table of Contents

Introduction – A New Kind of Advisor

- The average financial advice client is getting older
- Competition and the internet have commoditized many services
- Clients are demanding to see value for the fees they pay
- The 'new' advisor will provide services that tie life goals to financial strategies
- We call this 'Life-First Advice', to reflect the holistic and comprehensive nature of such an approach

If you were to imagine your practice 10 years from now, what would it look like? How would your clients' needs have changed? What role would you play in their lives? Would you still have a role?

It seems evident that our industry is at an inflection point. Traditional approaches to financial advice are likely to diminish and a new kind of advisor will emerge.

We believe this new kind of advisor will be what we call the 'Life-First Advisor' – someone who takes an approach that goes beyond financial planning and money management to the life issues that drive financial decisions. It's a term that not only describes what such advisors do for clients but also a way for these advisors to differentiate themselves in the market.

The Life-First approach recognizes that client needs change as they move from wealth accumulation to wealth conversion, wealth protection and, ultimately, wealth transference. Client planning requirements are evolving away from 'single-need' solutions such as investment management or tax planning and towards integrated solutions that demand a truly holistic approach.

Yes, there are already 'holistic advisors' out there, but we don't believe they are truly holistic. For some, holistic advice is a purely financial approach, defined in terms of looking at the client's overall financial picture. Others take a life planning approach and focus on the psychological or emotional aspects of money.

But these two approaches used in isolation from each other are not holistic and on their own present problems. A focus on emotions can be much appreciated by the client, but they may find it hard to articulate what the advisor actually does for them. The purely financial approach can fail to differentiate the advisor's value proposition from that of other advisors – clients assume you will look at all aspects of their financial situation in any case, and most advisors would claim that they do.

The Life-First approach combines both of these to provide truly holistic advice.

Staying ahead of the curve

A restaurant we know has thrived for 50 years under the same family management. Hundreds of other restaurants have come and gone in that time, but this dining spot continues to attract customers through good times and bad.

Asked why he has been so successful, the owner told us: "Simple – we've probably undergone two dozen style changes since we've been open. It's not so much that the food is good, but the fact that we've been able to anticipate the changing tastes of our clientele before everyone else. The restaurant industry is full of examples of good restaurants that have fallen out of favour simply because their owners rested on their laurels."

This example is seldom followed in the financial advice business, where firms typically stick with what's worked in the past.

But when you consider the pace of change in most professions and industries today, it would be short-sighted to think the global financial advice industry would be immune. We are already seeing the impact of 'robo-advisors', Google and direct low-cost providers on the way clients seek advice and what they will pay for.

Traditionally, investment and financial planning focused on positioning the client for the future. Clients looked to retirement as the incentive to save for tomorrow. That future has arrived, and today's client has different needs than a decade ago.

A maturing consumer is moving from the accumulation stage to more immediate concerns, such as:

- Will I have enough?
- What kind of life can I lead now that I'm retiring?
- How do I plan for the day-to-day life issues I'll face as I get older?

The fact is, client needs change as demographics, technology and the wider economy evolve. To satisfy those needs and stay ahead of your competitors you need to be flexible and responsive, while continually examining the value you bring to clients, prospects, target markets and centers-of-influence.

The Japanese business philosophy of *kaizen* holds that successful businesses make small, daily improvements in what they do so as to maintain their success. They never take their success for granted by just sitting with their formula. In fact, change is both expected and incorporated into planning. Instead of saying "if it ain't broke, don't fix it", consider what might break in the future.

In pondering change, many advice firms presume it's just a question of updating the positioning or the delivery of advice. This makeover approach is akin to rearranging the deck chairs on the Titanic.

The reality is that the service clients want to buy has changed. In short, the success of your practice in the future will depend on the moves you make today to stay ahead of the curve.

Why Life-First Advice suits changing times

If the future that your advice was directing people to has arrived, how do you reposition yourself?

Life-First Advisors help clients transition to the next phase of life. Using a 'life-based' instead of a 'money-based' approach, the advisor talks to clients about their needs, concerns, opportunities and goals before moving to financial solutions.

Because the nature of the discussion focuses more on the life and emotional issues that clients face, the advisor moves from being purely a financial counsellor to a mentor, a coach, educator and catalyst for change.

In other words, you become the *primary advisor* in clients' lives, one who understands their key concerns and the financial resources available to serve them.

This involves a transition away from transaction-based compensation to a fee-based approach, to ensure the services the advisor provides are in total alignment with the client's needs and interests. Clients then understand that they are paying the advisor for a coaching and planning role rather than for their ability to pick stocks or forecast markets.

Finally, and in contrast to many of their counterparts, Life-First Advisors take a strategic or 'passive' approach to portfolio asset allocation. They manage their clients' nest eggs based on where clients are in their lives rather than on what the market is doing at any given time.

The need is already there

In the wealth accumulation phase, clients typically sought advice from different specialist professionals related to their investment, insurance, tax and other material needs. But moving to wealth conversion, wealth protection and wealth transfer, they want someone who can look at the whole picture.

This is the holistic approach and it no longer carries the stigma of being 'too far out there' for seasoned investment professionals. In fact, whether or not advisors want to offer holistic solutions, research shows there is a clear and growing need for professionals who can tie financial issues to life issues.

In research by Vanguard and Morningstar in 2015, a client's return increased by more than 2 percent if the advisor provided comprehensive financial planning. Further research by Mercer pegged this increase at 2.27 percent[1].

A 2011 study on client behavior released in the US found that those clients who received 'holistic' advice were more likely to stay with their advisors, provide referrals and view the advisor's service levels positively[2].

A study published in 2012 found that those advisors who took a holistic 'wealth management' approach had more than double the assets under administration of investment specialists and almost four times the annual income. Better yet, they were able to accomplish this with less than half the number of clients serviced by a typical investment advisor[3].

Understanding the role that emotion plays in client decision-making, Life-First Advisors adapt their client communication to suit. Using the process of 'Life-First Discovery', advisors improve their knowledge of the client and use that to build a realistic roadmap for their future. This becomes an integral part of their positioning with clients, their branding in the marketplace and their differentiation strategy.

---

[1] David Barton, Mercer Investments, US, quoted in Kiplinger's Finance, June 2015

[2] ByAllAccounts, "Providing Holistic Advice through Account Aggregation," Financial Advisor Magazine, October 2012

[3] Cerulli Associates, 2012

Becoming a Life-First Advisor

In this book we provide the roadmap to becoming a Life-First Advisor. Our focus is not on investment management or financial plans. Nor is this yet another practice management book. Think of this as your guide to positioning yourself as the 'advisor of the future', one who will survive as our industry goes through a paradigm shift.
We will explore:

- Communicating with clients.
- Learning about clients using Life-First Discovery.
- Differentiating yourself using a Life-First Advisor value proposition.
- Marketing your unique approach to advice.
- Developing client contact programs.
- Using social media to build your business.
- The role of education events.
- Managing your practice effectively to give more time to clients.

Heart and head

Bob Veres, a respected commentator on the financial advice industry in the United States, once counseled advisors to "become a pioneer in the process of connecting financial affairs with deeper human values. Financial advice has become the most practical of professions ... but that is going to change so quickly that if you blink you will miss it!".

'Wealth' is your clients' ability to do what they want, when they want and how they want. It goes beyond money and addresses the most basic of human needs:

- To survive.
- To be safe.
- To belong and be needed.
- To feel good about ourselves.
- To live the life of our dreams.

Clients today demand more. They are demanding a partnership that revolves around their life and not just around their money. Every stage of life requires financial preparation and adjustment – and your clients know this. As a result, clients are going to turn these matters over to someone who has gained a clear picture of where they've been and are, and to someone who can help them develop a clear picture of where they're going.

In the future, our business will be about teaching, coaching – both strategically and inspirationally – and connecting with the lives of our clients.

That is what the Life-First Advisor does.

If you're willing to adopt this approach to financial advice and develop the necessary skills to communicate effectively, clients will find their way to you.

Barry LaValley
Principal, The Retirement Advisor
Vancouver

David Haintz
Principal, Global Adviser Alpha Pty Ltd
Melbourne

1 | Redefining Your Role

- **Five megatrends are changing the nature of what clients expect**
- **Advisors will take on new roles in the lives of their clients, increasingly becoming partners, mentors and 'coaches'**
- **The Life-First Advisor's brand will be based on their 'relationship' with the client, rather than the work performed on their financial affairs – *what* they do, rather than *how* they do it**

Do most of your clients understand what it is you do? Do they view you as a 'finance' person, or as a 'trusted advisor'? In the future, will they be willing to pay you for what they think you do?

"Look, I sell financial advice", one advisor told us. "My clients expect that I will provide them with financial planning and investment advice. I'm not going to get into anything about life planning or the soft issues. It just isn't me".

Many advisors feel the same way. "Oh, I could never talk to my clients about their 'legacy' and what their values are", said another. "You can only go so far prying into personal information about a client."

To be fair, many clients don't expect their advisor to talk to them about their hopes, dreams and feelings. After all, most of the marketing and advertising out there suggests the job of advisors is to talk about 'financial stuff'.

Yet, look at the relationship you have with your top clients – clients who have been with you for years, or with whom you've developed a great relationship. Have you noticed how your conversations with them often fall outside financial planning?

What if you could bottle that part of the relationship and sell it in the marketplace? In other words: stop marketing your services as an advisor who basically does what everyone else tries to do anyway and start marketing what you really do.

In fact, that's what clients are looking for – even if they don't know it. They want personal interaction with a trusted advisor. They want an advisor who can teach them the things they need to know about their money and their life.

Why not market your ability to help them with the things they value the most? This is why we developed the Life-First Approach.

The role of the advisor must change to meet the needs of aging clients who are moving from asset accumulation to a search for life meaning. Sure, advisors will continue to sell financial products or provide investment and insurance advice. But this advice will be part of a much bigger picture and placed in the context of the client's life.

Let's start by looking at the big-picture changes that are affecting the advice industry.

Five megatrends

The aging population, the growing importance of women as clients, the changing regulatory environment, new compensation structures for advisors and the 'disruption' of industries and businesses in the internet era are megatrends that are all contributing to the emergence of the modern advisor.

Trend 1 – An aging clientele

Every day 10,000 Americans turn 65. Similar population 'waves' are occurring in Australia, Canada, New Zealand, South Africa and the United Kingdom.

Today, it's estimated the average age of a client in the US with investable assets of $1 million or more is 62[4], while in Australia the average age of a superannuation fund 'millionaire' is 59[5].

You've likely spent much of your career helping people save for this day – their retirement. Like many others in the industry, your focus has probably been on 'accumulation', with investment advice an increasingly prominent part of your role.

While investment management will remain an important element of what you do, it won't be sufficient if you are to meet all the planning needs of an aging clientele.

As clients move their sights towards issues such as protecting their lifestyle or converting their savings into income for retirement, the type of planning they need changes. No longer are their goals in the distant future – their life needs, concerns and opportunities are now more immediate.

And they are changing, too, as people. We know most people tend to become more 'emotional' as they age. This is partly because of hormonal changes, partly due to the perspective born from accumulated life experience and perhaps also because of the growing sense of our own mortality.

This has implications for the way advisors should communicate with clients. Communication that respects the role emotion plays in decision-making will resonate with older clients.

Opportunities: This opens up a window for advisors to help clients understand and plan for the later-life issues that have financial consequences as well as personal ones. The advisor's role here is as educator and catalyst.

Advisors can become 'transition' specialists, helping clients understand the major issues they will face in their later years and prompting them to address the key issues associated with each of these life changes.

---

[4] Spectrem Group, 2015
[5] Australian Bureau of Statistics, 2014

The advisor can also help clients find the information they need to gain a better understanding of all the issues associated with aging, not just the financial ones. This doesn't you stop talking about money – it just means money discussions become more closely related to 'life'.

Advisors can act as a guide, providing information through newsletters and websites, and in seminars and workshops. They don't have to be the expert in all areas – but they need to be able to point the client in the right direction.

Trend 2 – The growing importance of women as clients

Women currently make up about 50 percent of the adult population but they will become an increasingly important market for financial advice as the population ages.

When you consider that 60 percent of all American women over 65 are single, widowed or divorced, you begin to see the change that will occur in the financial services industry as the wave of baby boomers reaches and surpasses this age.

While it's estimated that women currently control about 60 percent of the wealth in the US, this figure is forecast to rise to 75 percent by 2020[6].

There has been a lot of research on how women look at money and we know that, from a planning perspective, they're more likely to take an objective-based approach than a purely financial one. While the financial goal for a man might be to 'beat the index', a woman is more likely to say her goal is to 'protect our lifestyle'.

Meanwhile, just 30 percent of financial advisors are women – a number that hasn't changed significantly in 10 years – and many of the marketing and communications approaches in this industry are still aimed at a predominantly male clientele.

Too often advisors lament the loss of a client when a widow moves money from one firm to another advisor. "I can't believe my client would take her money and move it", one advisor said. "We had great performance in her funds and I always had such a good relationship with her husband before he passed away".

---

[6] US Census, Breakdown of Households, 2013

Opportunities: Advisors who provide a service that meets the needs of both men and women, and whose marketing and communications take into account the differences between these two sets of clients, will benefit from these demographic changes.

Pay attention to how you communicate. Men tend to be drawn to left-brain, finance-based approaches while women tend to be more right-brain, life-goal oriented. Many women respond better to a coaching, consultative approach than a purely advisory approach.

This will not only affect how you articulate your value proposition but also, at a practical level, how you conduct discovery and the focus you take in the overall planning process.

Review your 'book' to assess the risk of losing assets because you don't have relationships with the spouses of your male clients. Involve spouses in planning discussions.

Develop programs to market to female prospects and ensure your marketing material, education seminars and other communications appeal to both men and women. Ensure everyone understands your life-based approach.

Remember the importance of relationship management, particularly with your female clients. You may have had relationships with male clients based on a shared interest in investment management, but for most women investment management is neither a game nor a hobby. They want a relationship with their advisor that's relevant to their lives. We'll talk more about this in chapter 12.

The good thing is that paying more attention to relationship management will help you with both male and female clients.

Trend 3 – A changing regulatory environment

In the wake of the global financial crisis (GFC) governments around the world took steps to address professional accountability, transparency and oversight in the financial services industry.

In the US, Australia and Canada, new rules covering financial advice required advisors to know more about their clients than ever before. Advisors were put on notice that they must meet the highest standards of transparency, and that they must be cognizant of their 'duty' to those they serve.

If advisors are to act in the best interests of clients, as these new regulations demand, they will have to go further in client discovery than simply understanding financial issues and personal balance sheets. To achieve a full understanding of their client, advisors will need to come to grips with the emotional issues that often lie behind client decisions.

In this environment, there will be added impetus to expand their roles as educators, with financial literacy an important element of client care. While many do this now, the focus tends to be more on 'money' than on the life context within which money must be viewed.

Opportunities: These new requirements to fully understand clients underline the need for a discovery process that helps clients see the larger life issues that are the backdrop to sound decision-making.

A deeper discovery process not only gives the advisor greater knowledge and understanding of a client, it also helps clients gain a better understanding of the advisor's role.

Clients would be well served if advisors had a good appreciation of behavioral finance and how clients think, act and make decisions. Advisors should be able to work with clients to moderate their emotional and cognitive biases and to adapt to those biases that are 'hard wired' into clients.

If clients then see their advisors in the role of coach, educator, mentor and even 'project manager', they are more likely to see the true value the advisor provides.

Trend 4 – New compensation structures

Advisors are also under pressure to change the way they charge for what they do. Post-GFC regulations specifically addressed the issue of transparency of fee structure and clients around the world are becoming more aware of how fees are charged. They are increasingly likely to ask questions about the value they receive for those fees.

The future is likely to include downward pressure on commissions (set by third-party product manufacturers) and an increase in fee-based advice (agreed between client and advisor).

There's already a global trend away from commissions. In Australia, advisors are no longer able to charge commissions <u>on investment advice</u>, while a recent decision by regulators in the UK outlaws commissions for recommending specific products to clients.

In the US, a 2015 study found that the fee-based advisor is the fastest growing financial services channel – rising 40 percent since 2005[7].

Opportunities: The increase in consumer focus on advisor 'value' is likely to prompt the industry to examine how to demonstrate and communicate that value. Even if advisors don't change what they do for clients, they'll certainly have to change how they explain what they do, to make their practice stand out.

Enlightened advisors have the opportunity to redefine what an advisor does for their client in terms that differ from the current value proposition. Meet this challenge and you can become the standard by which other advisors will be judged.

We believe you should become the kind of advisor clients 'didn't know they were looking for'.

That means the way you provide advice has to look different. It's hard to provide a different approach to investment management, tax planning or financial planning because they've become commoditized. These are just the how of financial planning; you can set yourself apart by defining what you do for clients in the context of their life goals.

Changing fee structures support this by allowing you to be compensated for the real work you do with clients as coach, mentor, educator and project manager. Clients will soon understand that it's these roles that provide them with real value for the fees they pay.

---

[7] "Fee-based, discount brokerage and online channels to grow", Wealth Management Magazine, US, July 2016

Now the advisor and client can truly be on the same side of the table, regardless of the short-term gyrations of investment markets.

Trend 5 – Online disruption

Ten years ago, if you wanted to book a vacation you went to a travel agent. Today, you'd more likely book online. Think about how you buy books, music and consumer goods … If the internet has been a game changer in every other industry, why would financial advice be immune?

Your competition is no longer the other advisors in your marketplace. Every day your clients browse the internet for news and knowledge and to connect to the world. A 2013 study estimated that the average American spends 23 hours a week on the internet and that two hours of that time involves their personal finances[8]. Your client is exposed each and every day to advice and commentary, solicited or not.

Clients can conduct transactions online, and they can obtain basic financial planning and investment advice without ever having to speak with a licensed advisor.

We are seeing the growth of the 'robo-advisor' and access to lower-cost transactions and advice. Providers such as Betterment and Vanguard are providing clients with access to advice as part of their offering for a small fee. Schwab offers basic financial planning at no cost.

Advisors will argue a computer can't do what they do, and we strongly agree. But if clients don't understand what an advisor actually does – if advisors don't successfully communicate what they do – then people can be forgiven for thinking they don't need a professional advisor in the online world.

Opportunities: Advisors need to focus on the things the internet can't provide to clients and enlist the internet in connecting with the market. Use your web presence and social media to communicate the real value of the advice you provide.

---

[8] The Buntin Group and Survey Sampling International, 2013

The key is to stay 'above the line' – focusing your message on what you do for people emotionally rather than just what you do for their money (below the line). This is a concept we will revisit throughout this book.

Social media will be very important, and we discuss this in a later chapter. It will likely become the foundation of your marketing programs, client contact strategies and center-of-influence communications.

The key is to understand the challenges and opportunities social networking provides, both from a client contact perspective and as a marketing and name recognition tool. Your opportunity is to use your internet presence to show people why you are different. In fact, it will help you deliver services downline once the trust is developed.

The internet will not replace the value of face-to-face and the role that it plays in building trust. While some may say that using Skype or other online meeting tools will save time for both you and the client, consider the price you may pay in the development of trust.

The new advisor

Clients are getting older and it would be short-sighted to suggest they have the same needs today as they had when they were younger.

In the accumulation phase, clients required advisors who could help them make sense of the multitude of investment and savings options to help them build a nest egg for the future. The advisor role was often that of an investment advisor. In fact, many advisors still have the title 'Investment Advisor' on their business cards and focus their marketing on their ability to manage money and mitigate risk.

But as clients get older their needs turn from wealth accumulation to wealth protection, conversion of wealth to income and, ultimately, wealth transfer to the next generation.

Investment advice, while still necessary, becomes less important in the overall scheme of things as clients deal with health issues, pending retirement, the 'empty nest', along with many other aspects of aging.

As these clients transition to a new phase of life, they will have more questions than answers and advisors will need to become:

- **Educators** helping clients understand the key issues that need to be planned for.

- **Mentors** supporting clients who are uncertain about the choices they face with both their money and their lives.

- **Coaches** keeping people on track and accountable.

- **Catalysts** helping shape client decision making.

- **Project managers** liaising with other professionals, and overseeing implementation of strategies – saving clients time and inconvenience.

We'll look at these roles in more depth later in this book.

Wealth management itself hasn't changed. It's just that the maturing client needs different elements in a wealth plan. Advisors will still deal with two basic elements when they provide advice: the resources the client has, and how to achieve the client's goals.

As one advisor put it: "The hardest clients to help are the ones who have no goals. If the client just wants to make money, that doesn't provide a standard by which to judge the value of your assistance. Help clients to frame a picture of their ideal retirement, or of providing for their children, so you then have goals to work towards".

We are on the verge of a paradigm shift in how advisors work with their clients. The Life-First Advisor recognizes that the value he or she brings to clients actually changes the way clients are viewed, the sort of advice delivered, and how a business is developed.

Outcomes-based advice

In 2007 a client decided to move his portfolio to a new advisor who he felt would better manage his retirement funds. This client had $4 million in the portfolio and had just retired at age 65.

The new advisor repositioned the portfolio to take advantage of an expected upswing in the market. They undertook all the due diligence involved in understanding the client's risk tolerance and made investments that fit the client's profile.

In the following 18 months the client lost almost half of his portfolio in the GFC and had to return to work. If fault could be assigned, it might fall on both the client and advisor, who were scrambling to understand the new reality of volatile markets and economic upheaval.

The advisor's goal was to provide a return on investment for the client. In fact, one of the reasons he gained this new client was his offer of a 'second opinion'. The client may have needed a second opinion, but not on how his money was being managed. Rather, the fresh look should have been on whether the client's financial resources met his life needs and goals.

This is objective-based or outcomes-based financial advice.

In the past, advisors tended to work 'below the line' and position financial products and services as the goal of their interaction with clients. (see chapter 4 for more on "above the line/below the line"). The modern Life-First Advisor is more concerned about providing outcomes-based advice.

As we've outlined, this means tying life concerns, opportunities, needs and goals to the financial strategies needed to accomplish them. Richer conversations with clients that help both the advisor and client understand the true issues will be the main tools in this work.

Those advisors who are able to reach deep into their client's heads and hearts to uncover these will certainly earn the fees they charge. Their role in their clients' lives will become transformational.

The Life-First Advisor ...

- Acknowledges their clientele is aging and needs are moving away from accumulation towards wealth protection, conversion and transfer
- Develops relationships with clients to become a coach, educator, mentor, project manager and catalyst
- Understands the planning and communication needs of both men and women
- Has a transparent approach to fees

2 | The Intuitive Advisor

- Effective communication is at the heart of the Life-First process
- It is important to understand how clients think, act and make decisions
- The Life-First Advisor understands the difference between the left and right brain
- They also understand the role of emotion in decision-making. Story telling is not just a way to learn, it is the way we learn

An investment advisor at a major firm was putting together a six-page client brochure. His goal was to provide potential clients an overview of what he does and why they should use him as their financial advisor.

The centerfold of the brochure was to be a description of his 12-step investment selection process. As his consultants, we asked him why he had so many steps. His response was that his clients would be impressed that he was so thorough in his due diligence.

Do clients really need to know an advisor has a 12-step investment process? Arguably, most would be comforted to know he at least has some process for making his recommendations and a few might want to know how many steps he takes. But even fewer would be interested in a 'deep dive'.

Ask yourself, "What do I really need to communicate effectively to my client? What is my role in their life and how do I use the communications methods at my disposal to reinforce that role?"

Many advisors would say it's their knowledge of the technical aspects of their craft that sets them apart. Yet it's their ability to reach their clients, prospects and centers-of-influence that, ultimately, determines their success.

While it's important for advisors to understand markets, tax planning and financial planning issues, it's equally important they understand and can communicate with their clients.

It doesn't matter how much you know if the client isn't listening. Yet we see it all the time: advisors using jargon, buzzwords and stilted language, assuming that clients and prospects have the same knowledge they do, and not realizing that what's important to the advisor may not be as important to the listener.

At what point do clients stop thinking about their investments as facts, figures and numbers and start to think about them in terms of their relationship to life issues? Probably a lot sooner than most advisors are willing to concede.

The important 'client conversation' is the one that takes place in their brain, not yours.

What is effective communication?

At its core, the Life-First approach is really a communications strategy. Communicating with your clients is not just a way to relate to them, it is what you do as a Life-First Advisor.

As a Life-First Advisor, everything about your message will be aimed at how the client thinks, acts and makes decisions. You'll get into your client's shoes, speak their language and focus on their issues.

On the surface, the communications process between advisor and client seems straightforward. The advisor explains to a client why a course of action is in their best interest, the client thinks about what the advisor says and then makes a decision.

Simple. But how effective is communication if it doesn't resonate with the receiver?

Picture another advisor creating a marketing brochure. The advisor writes about her experience and education, her investment process and her dedication to good service (leaving half the space for all the compliance material she has to insert). What she doesn't do is address the client's needs or interests.

Advisors make a leap of faith that the client or prospect will absorb every word as important. The challenge is that the audience may not be ready to 'hear' your message.

Think about it this way: when a radio station sends out its signal, it has an effect only on those sets tuned to the right frequency to receive the message. A connection needs to be established to enable the communication to be received. And in our business you are communicating with someone not at someone.

Let's talk 'brain science'

To help you understand how to build a communications strategy that resonates with clients – while also giving your business a point of difference – let's consider some basic 'brain science' principles. How do clients' brains actually work? There are a few key things to understand.

The brain has no outside view of the world. It only has an internal view based on its previous experience.

When the brain is presented with new information, it searches back though its own experiences to find a place to analyze or 'file' this information. If it can't find a previous experience that relates, it will either discard the information or misfile it.

For example, if you say to a client, "I am an investment advisor", their brain will process that in terms of what it already understands about investment advisors – for good or ill. This is why you must describe what you do in your own terms.

The brain doesn't like to work. Our brains run on glucose. The more you have to use the thinking or problem-solving part of the brain – also called the 'left brain' or prefrontal cortex – the less capacity you have to pay attention or use 'fluid' intelligence, the type of intelligence that allows us to entertain 'out of the box' thinking and new ideas.

Generally, when the brain is tired, or out of glucose in the problem-solving part of the brain, it will 'check out' and stop processing information. The same can happen if the information presented is too complex, too technical or just looks like a lot of work to go through.

When you communicate, consider whether you're in danger of putting the receiver's brain to sleep or asking it to work harder than it wants to.

The brain craves structure. The more structure it perceives, the easier it is for it to file information and pay attention to your message. Dale Carnegie was famous for this advice on making presentations: "Tell 'em what you're going to say, say it, then tell 'em what you said!".

Since the brain likes things to be easy, you can help the communications process by making sure you structure things in a way that helps the brain. When you lay out a message in a presentation, make sure you don't leave the listening brain trying to figure out where you're going.

What's more, the need for structure increases as clients get older. Psychologists use 'continuity theory' to explain how we view our world as we age, and the perception of structure is an important part of that – older clients begin to crave it as a way of feeling more comfortable.

Left brain v right brain

You've probably heard people speak about the left and right brain. More than pop psychology, this refers to the different roles of different parts of the brain, as mapped by scientists.

Essentially, the cerebral cortex can be divided into two halves, the left brain and the right brain. Put very simply, the left brain, or pre-frontal cortex, is the logical part of the brain while the right brain is the emotional center.

The left brain actually sits on top of the right brain, which makes these labels a bit of a misnomer. And no one is totally right-brain or left-brain dominant – some people are considered 'whole brain' processors.

While we generalize by saying the left brain is logical and the right brain emotional, in fact both sides of the brain are capable of reacting to left-brain and right-brain information. Sitting between the two is the corpus callosum, which contains millions of connectors that move information between left and right – sending electrochemical signals to specific areas of the brain responsible for deciphering each message.

Our brains take in data from our senses and then digitize the information and send it to the sensory cortex. Next it's broken down, analyzed and compared to similar patterns of information already stored in memory.

At the same time, the area of the brain responsible for our feelings, hopes, dreams and emotions provides input into the analysis.

Because the left brain and right brain are wired together, it's difficult to separate out some of the specific functions. But Roger Sperry, who won a Nobel Prize for his work on left-brain and right-brain reasoning, was able to look at how the functions of each hemisphere operate on their own by observing patients whose corpus callosum had been severed during surgery.

Sperry concluded that the two modes of thinking in humans – verbal and non-verbal – are located in the left and right brains respectively, representing two completely different and competing views of the world.

Here is how researchers have differentiated between the interpretations found in each hemisphere, based on Sperry's work:

Left Brain v Right Brain

Left-Brain Function	Right-Brain Function
Uses Logic	Uses feeling
Detail oriented	Big Picture oriented
"Facts Rule!"	"Imagination Rules!"
Words and language	Symbols and images
Past and present	Present and future
Math and Science	Philosophy and religion
Can comprehend	Can "get it"
Knowing	Believing
Acknowledges	Appreciates
Order/Pattern perception	Spatial perception
Knows object's name	Knows object's function
Reality based	Fantasy based
Forms strategies	Presents possibilities
Practical	Impetuous
Safe	Risk-Taking

Source: Dan Eden, "Left-brain, Right-brain", used by permission of author

To return to a concept we talked about earlier, you could consider an 'above the line' approach (the why of what you do for a client) to be right-brain related and your 'below the line' work (the what and the how) as related to the left brain.

This is why it's important to connect the dots for clients. If you tell them you're a Life-First Advisor, define what that means for them in terms that relate to both the right and the left brain. Include the 'and here is why this is important to you' part of the conversation.

Relating to your client's right brain

Your clients can relate to you in their right brain or their left. But if you don't engage them emotionally, it's the left brain that's likely to process and analyze the information you provide – deciding which information the right brain needs.

The logical brain judges as it tries to analyze the communication. If the client has any skepticism, this is where it comes from.

When you relate to a client emotionally rather than logically it sets up a different dynamic. Your client isn't judging you as much as reaching out to relate to you. Here are some differences between relating to your client on the logical and emotional sides of their brain:

Relating to your client's brain

Left brain	Right brain
Financial Planning	Teaching
Investing	Communicating
Income planning	Counseling
Tax	Coaching
Analysis	Supporting
Performance	Problem solving
Insurance illustrations	Intuition
Acronyms	Mentoring
Jargon	Guiding
Implementation	Motivating

So, *Why* the Life-first advisor practices the Life-first approach is to relate to the client's right brain. The *What* and the *How* that advisor does it is by relating to the client's left brain.

Environment has a lot to do with whether someone is likely to favour their left or right brain. For example, if a businessman leaves work and becomes a caregiver, it's quite likely he'll use right-brain thinking more than previously.

Both men and women tend to become more right-brain oriented as they get older and focus on lifestyle issues such as retirement, self-actualization, mortality and health. This is partly due to a decrease in testosterone production on the male side. Men become more emotional as they get older, whether they care to admit it or not.

The role of emotion

The role of emotion in decision-making can't be underestimated. Emotion guides our behavior and is generally the ultimate 'screen' before we act. It is the highway on which your communication moves through to a client's decision-making center.

Neuroscientists tell us our brains don't make decisions logically but emotionally. In fact, did you know the logical left brain actually has no decision-making ability? Think about it – that means we are one of the few businesses to speak to the wrong side of the brain when we try to demonstrate capability.

It's a misconception, however, that emotion is found only in the right brain. Sperry noted in his Nobel Lecture in 1981: "Unlike other aspects of cognitive function, emotions have never been readily confinable to one hemisphere – emotional effects tend to spread rapidly to involve both hemispheres."

So an advisor's discussion of emotional issues in the client's life can be a left-brain discussion, such as how the investment performance of a portfolio will help the client reach a stated goal. The client is emotionally engaged because reaching the goal is important.

However, a right-brain discussion probably created the goal in the first place. Why is that goal important? What's the emotional need behind the numbers? How will the client feel if they achieve the goal?

That makes context important in both communication and the decision-making process.

Content v context

Clients may listen but not 'hear' you if they're not emotionally engaged. They become engaged when you provide them with context – telling them 'what's in it for you'.

If you're just providing content, you won't flick the switch in their brain that gives you their full attention. Unfortunately, many advisors miss the role that context plays when they communicate, saying things like:

"My clients are sophisticated investors – they just want the bottom line and not any of this airy, soft stuff"

"I don't have time to get into their emotions – I'm a professional financial advisor and they'll lose respect for me if I start talking about feelings"

"I'm a CFA talking to other CFAs – we all talk the same language. I don't need to turn on any emotional light switches with this group"

In fact, our brains are programmed to reach out to others at the sub-cognitive level. Human interaction is a 'conversation' that exists even before verbal communication begins.

When you sit down with a client an unseen pathway is created between your emotional center and theirs by the brain's 'mirror neurons'. Mirror neurons read emotion. So, for example, we are more likely to respond positively to someone when they send out 'happy' or optimistic signals.

As an advisor, you're trying to 'look inside' your client, and they're doing the same – trying to look inside you. Wouldn't it make sense to demonstrate the kind of behavior that will help them understand who you are, how you can help them and whether they can trust you?

The oxytocin response

Trust is a word frequently used in our business. But trust doesn't come from the words you say or the services and accreditations you advertise. Trust is in most part a chemical reaction in your client's hormonal system – it's generated internally, not externally.

It comes from the oxytocin response, or the basic human bonding mechanism. The pituitary gland produces a hormone called oxytocin when you feel good about someone, flooding the connectors that work on memory and decision-making. Mothers bonding with newborn babies and 'love at first sight' are examples of this response at work.

At the same time, our brain's reward center releases a neurotransmitter called dopamine, the 'happy hormone' that is responsible for our sense of wellbeing and happiness.

If people are going to trust you, they have to feel good about you. That relationship is developed 'above the line', not below the line. Yet most advisors would use a below-the-line explanation to describe why clients trust them.

So, think of your communication with a client at two levels: the verbal, visual and tactile communication that can be controlled through actions and words, and the non-verbal communication that flows from emotion. You're communicating with someone both 'head to head' and 'heart to heart'.

Often, advisors will describe how they create trust by "doing what we say we will do" or "always acting in the client's best interest". Those are examples of sustaining trust—not creating it!

Two types of intelligence

Another brain scientist, Raymond Catell, has identified two important elements of general intelligence: fluid and crystallized intelligence. These two types of intelligence are separate neural and mental systems that act in coordination.

Fluid intelligence describes our ability to solve new problems, learn new things or find order out of chaos.

Crystallized intelligence describes our ability to use the skills, knowledge and experience we already have.

One way to look at this is to think of your computer. Its' hard drive is a storage area that contains all the information entered since you started using it, while its random access memory, or RAM, is the 'thinking' part that allows it to perform many of its functions.

Crystallized intelligence is like the hard drive – it's the sum total of all the knowledge we've accumulated over time. What's there is there, including instructions that say, in the absence of any new direction, 'just do what you've always done'.

Fluid intelligence is like RAM. It can work with the information already on the hard drive but it can also add new information and programs. Fluid intelligence allows us to entertain new thinking. And the only way to ensure fluid intelligence has been engaged is to apply those right-brain concepts we talked about earlier.

Turning on switches

The light switch metaphor we used earlier has some foundation in neuroscience. If you were to look at a brain scan of someone receiving information, you'd see certain regions of the brain 'fire up' in response to the communications received and the thought process created.

All your communication should start with a very simple act: turning on the light switches in your client's head at the beginning of each discourse.

Think of the brain as a house with a number of rooms, each with a light switch. So, for example, you light the 'basement' when you talk about:

- Price-earnings multiples.
- Investment strategies.
- Insurance proposals.
- Efficient frontiers.
- Tax planning strategies.
- Estate planning.

However, you light the 'living room' when you talk about what those mean to clients in terms of:

- Their hopes.
- Their possibilities.
- Their family.
- Their fears and concerns.
- Their dreams.
- Their concept of 'self'.
- Their need for validation.

Any house needs a basement or foundations to support the living area, but the 'living room' is where life happens. The aim of financial strategies is to support the life needs, concerns, opportunities and goals of your clients. Therefore, your communication should start by understanding the emotional issues your clients think about.

It should also facilitate 'self-discovery' – helping clients have a better understanding of their own wants and needs.

This is because research on how the brain makes decisions shows that it operates more effectively if it can use its own fluid intelligence to draw conclusions.

So while it's true that clients may make decisions based on what an advisor says, the larger the decision to be made the more the client needs to process the information in their own head.

As an advisor, you have the ability to turn on left- or right-brain switches. Turn a left-brain switch on and you have activated a machine. Turn a right-brain switch on and you have activated a person.

Storytelling and the brain

We all know someone who made an impression on us because of a story they told. Neuroscience tells us that stories aren't merely one way we process information – they are *the* way we process information.

We have a need to put things into a narrative so the right brain can imbed the experience into long-term memory. We dream in stories, we think in stories and we are drawn to stories that engage us.

The brain actually creates stories on its own as it makes sense of the information with which it is bombarded. We are all familiar with the concept of 'self-talk' or the ongoing narrative we have with ourselves as we think about the information we receive. We use self-talk in an effort to organize our thoughts and focus on the issues we have to deal with. The concept of the mind map is an example of this effort to create order out of chaos.

When you tell stories, or encourage your client to develop a narrative, you're helping them organize and bundle information. This is why metaphors, analogies, testimonials and stories work so well in client communications.

Let's say you present your client with a strategy that will provide them with predictable cash flow over the life of their retirement. In their head, they'll translate that into something like, 'Let's see, that would mean we could afford a new boat'.

Your discovery process will also be more effective if you create an atmosphere where the client can tell stories that help both of you understand the issues more clearly.

Telling your own story

Clients will also relate to you better if you can tell them a personal story that helps them understand you. Some advisors say, "There's nothing about me I would want to tell a client – I don't really have a 'story'".

Everyone has a story! Consider your answers to these questions:

- What motivated you to become a financial advisor?

- Why do you do what you do, as opposed to something else?

- What were some of the earliest lessons about money that still influence you today?

- What is it that you like best about what you do?

- What are some of the ways you've made an impact on the clients you have worked with in the past?

Your story doesn't have to be long, but you should be ready and able to share some real emotion with a client or prospect.

Speaking to the brain and heart

Human beings are not computers. We don't just take in information, process it and react to it. In fact, the route your communications must take to reach the decision-making part of your client's brain is full of potholes and side roads.

Follow the right neurological path and you have a better chance of the client hearing your message in the way you intend.

You've probably heard a variation of the story of the new shoe salesman who was frustrated because he wasn't selling many pairs of shoes:

"I don't know what I'm doing wrong", he lamented to an older colleague after a particularly frustrating day. "I must have served 50 different people today who all looked like they wanted to buy shoes but I sold just two pairs!"

In company training, the young salesman had known more about how shoes were constructed than anyone else. He could talk about the various kinds of leather and shoe dyes that most manufacturers used.

"Not only that", he continued, "but I made sure the shoes they tried on fit properly and had them walk around the store just to make sure. And they still didn't buy!"

"Let me ask you", said the older salesman, "what are your customers buying when they buy shoes?"

Seeing his young friend's puzzled expression, he continued: "They're actually buying beauty and self-esteem. They're buying a sense of 'feeling good'. It's not the shoes that are important, it's how the shoes make them feel that matters".

Theoretically, shoe buyers should buy shoes because they fit properly and are made of good leather. On that basis, investors should buy stocks because an advisor has a 12-step stock selection process that identifies the best picks.

This is seldom the case. Clients don't always behave rationally because human beings don't always behave rationally. Most advisors believe their clients will respond to things that are logical simply because clients are intelligent and care about their own wellbeing.

The reason for this misconception is that many advisors believe our brains act in the same way as a computer. The advisor simply has to give an intelligent client the information and the client will compute that information and make a decision.

That isn't what happens at all. We process information based on what we already know and we base our decisions on how we see ourselves. It's not the numbers that make us feel good but what those numbers mean to our sense of well-being.

The Life-First Advisor ...

- Understands the need to relate to a client personally

- Moves the conversation to the right brain

- Uses their communication skills to encourage client self-discovery

- Recognizes that 'trust' comes from a heart-to-heart connection not just a 'head to head' one

3 | From Transaction to Transformation

- **Trusted advisors help clients deal with the emotional as well as financial implications of life changes**

- **The Life First Advisor coaches clients through important life transitions**

- **This changes the discussion from 'product' to planning**

- **Transition planning identifies possible life changes and builds an integrated strategy**

"It's funny what happens to you as you get older", one client said at a recent seminar. "I have a completely different view of my money than I used to have. I'm more worried right now about having a heart attack than I am about where the markets are going!"

We've always had life transitions and 'rites of passage'. It's just that, today, the baby boom generation is hitting the same big life transition at the same time. One American turns 65 every seven seconds. The clock ticks over for one Canadian and one Australian approximately every minute. As one commentator noted, "We're in the middle of the biggest mass mid-life crisis in history".

For the financial services industry, this requires a service offering that's radically different to the one presented over the past 20 years. The advice business will become a transition-management business because the vast majority of clients will need that kind of help.

Unexpected life transitions

Life happens. Over the decades, we encounter many challenges and lots of change. Obviously we don't know what, how or when. We do know, however, that there are likely to be emotional and financial implications from each life change. It's at these points that we'll seek the counsel of people we trust.

Most professional financial advisors are on solid ground when it comes to discussing the financial consequences of an unexpected life change. For people experiencing bereavement, one of the first calls outside family and friends may be to an insurance professional, for instance.

Advisors are called upon to help deal with divorce, financial windfalls and financial catastrophes. Much of the training you undertake as a financial planning professional prepares you to provide advice and counsel in difficult times.

Even so, you'll often be in 'reaction mode' when such an event occurs. Your client will ask you to do something because a life change has necessitated making a financial transaction of some sort. You give your client the facts and figures they require, but you may not be able to meet their emotional needs in dealing with change.

When clients need you most

On the face of it, the time an advisor is most needed would seem to be at these major turning points in life – arranging insurance for new parents, for example, or giving investment advice after an inheritance.

In fact, the time a client really needs their advisor is *before* a transition, if possible – when there's still time to put plans in place.

The most common changes that occur in the life of your clients are:

- Marriage
- Buying a home
- A new baby
- New job or promotion
- Sudden downsizing
- Marital change
- Retirement
- Health challenges
- Bereavement

Life changes make financial issues 'top of mind', altering them from something deep within the client's subconscious to a need that must be met. For a maturing client, life changes seem to come with increasing frequency, whether it's to do with health, work or family relationships.

Every time a client encounters a life-altering experience, there's an opportunity to create new plans and goals based on the new reality, and for the financial advisor to reinforce the relevance of what they do for the client.

Experiencing change

The transition from one stage of life to another can be difficult, as many retirees will attest. Have you ever wondered why some retirees make the transition easily while others struggle for years? Part of the answer comes from the way we process change in our lives.

William Bridges, a well-known expert on life change, has a simple way of looking at what happens when we undergo life change.

The Bridges Life Transition Model

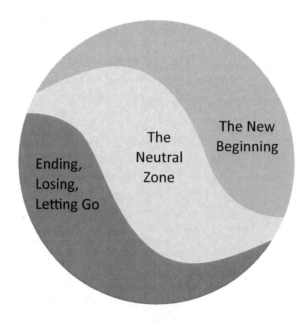

Source: *Managing Transitions: Making the Most of Change*, 2009

Bridges suggests the neutral zone can be a time of chaos and stress if the individual hasn't accepted the end of the previous phase and anticipated the arrival of the new phase. If your client hasn't begun planning for the next phase of life (for example, retirement), there's a risk the neutral zone will be chaotic[9].

If you sense a client is having difficulty because of a life event such as the death of spouse, retirement or job loss it may be because they're having difficulty moving out of the past and accepting their new life as it exists today.

In many cases, your act of caring can make it easier for them to talk about the issues.

Some life transitions have severe emotional and financial consequences that may feel difficult to bring up in conversation. Major health challenges, psychological issues, divorce and job loss are all life transitions that require both sensitivity and professional expertise.

A client won't normally start a conversation with, "I'm thinking about divorcing my wife and I want to go over my financial situation". The advisor isn't going to say in a meeting, "George, you look like you could use a psychiatrist. Here's a card."

This idea worries many financial advisors. "I'm not a psychologist or personal coach", said one. "My job is to talk about money issues and I'm going to stick to that."

Great, except the issue is not the money but the emotion around the transition event, as we discussed earlier. To bridge that gap advisors need to provide a 'safe' environment where clients feel comfortable sharing their concerns.

---

[9] Bridges, William, *Managing Transitions: Making the Most of Change*, 2009

Talking to clients about change

Your client has to understand the life transition discussion is a normal part of the financial planning process. Here's how a Life-First Advisor might address this:

"John, one of the benefits I can provide is my knowledge and expertise in helping you protect yourself and your family financially from the life changes that will happen in the future. In our ongoing discussions, I'll focus on some common life changes and events you may be concerned about in the future."

When you're helping a client accumulate assets for the future, your discussions often focus on the transactions that need to take place. What funds should you buy and when? What should you do about the technology stocks you own? Are you properly diversified to protect yourself from reversing stock markets? Those are all transaction-focused.

Transition-focus or life-stage planning moves away from a situation or product discussion and moves towards three key questions:

- Where are you now?

- Where will you be in the foreseeable future?

- Where do you want to be in the long term?

Transition planning is the identification of possible life transitions and the analysis of what strategies might be put in place to help the client take advantage of the transition or to ease the burden of the change.

Where can the advisor provide the most value for the client? While the answer to that question will be as varied as the number of clients you have, typically you can provide the most value by helping a client through a change.

Advisors will need to hone their skills in helping clients deal with changes in their lives. Clients won't normally entrust their inner feelings to someone who hasn't earned the right to listen or provide advice. However, if you show that you take an overall view of the client's life, not just a financial view, they will begin to see you in a different light.

Change is a right-brain issue

Think about what happens to a client when an unexpected life transition occurs. Let's say your client is suddenly given a buyout package from her job. She has been a successful executive with a stock option plan and a big salary; she has also been diligent in making regular contributions to her retirement savings and her investment portfolio. Financially, she has looked after herself with your help.

Now, at age 50, her world has changed and she faces the emotional challenges of losing her job. What is she going to do with her time? Will she ever work again or is her business career over? How will she replace the function her work performed in her life?

She isn't worried about financial planning at a time like this, even though clearly she will have to deal with her buyout package.

If you're aware of the basic changes your clients go through and have raised your antennae to the predictable changes, you can increase the value of your relationship with the client by 'being there' at such a time of transition.

The advisors who can make a difference in the life of a client in non-financial areas are those who have established a level of trust and confidence with clients that goes beyond money.

If you've taken a comprehensive life planning approach from the outset, it's only natural for the client to consider you an important resource for advice and counsel when a significant life change occurs. They'll want all the advice they can access.

For those advisors who believe they need only update their client information once or twice a year, where do your clients turn when something unforeseen happens? You don't have to be on the phone every month, like an ambulance chaser looking for accidents, but a regular communication schedule keeps you in the client's mind.

By staying in touch, you remain relevant. A life change event gives you the opportunity to provide pertinent information on matters that are very personal to the client, at a time when the client really needs the advice.

Ultimately, your clients need your services on *their* schedule – not yours.

The financial impacts

Most of the predictable life changes have financial implications. The opportunity for an advisor to reposition themselves as a 'Life CFO' comes by making the client aware of these.

Approaching life transitions as a financial issue, first, gives you the right to carry the discussion further and puts you in a position to provide your client with some important non-financial information they'll also find valuable.

The Life-First Advisor and life transitions

Death of a spouse	<ul><li>Acting as a friend instead of an advisor</li><li>Addressing their fears openly</li><li>Taking on some tasks that will give your client time to grieve</li><li>Providing information and assistance on unfamiliar areas they need to deal with</li><li>Performing same roles with extended family if needed</li></ul>	<ul><li>Wills, probate etc.</li><li>Insurance policies</li><li>Employment issues</li><li>Inheritance</li><li>Burial and final expenses</li><li>Financial planning for remaining spouse</li><li>Disposal of assets</li><li>Loss of income</li><li>Change in financial situation</li></ul>
Critical illness	<ul><li>Address issues openly if client asks</li><li>Provide assistance and comfort for family</li><li>Take away financial management concerns</li><li>Be sensitive to need for lifestyle money in terminal illness situation</li></ul>	<ul><li>Income replacement</li><li>Insurance issues</li><li>Asset management</li><li>Health-care costs</li><li>Change in work situation</li></ul>
Divorce	<ul><li>Be a friend, then an advisor</li><li>Provide unemotional, rational counsel</li><li>Recognize and provide information on lifestyle adjustments</li></ul>	<ul><li>Inventory of assets</li><li>Disposal of assets</li><li>Managing settlements</li><li>Day-to-day financial management concerns</li><li>Tax implications</li><li>Income changes</li></ul>

Job transfer	• Reaffirming portability of your relationship and plan • Information on new locale	• Income changes • Moving expenses • Standard of living changes • Insurance changes
Job promotion	• Consider that there may be some uncertainty or insecurity • Changes in lifestyle • Increase in stress level	• Income changes • Managing new assets • Reworking financial plan • Insurance changes • Tax planning
Job loss	• Understanding emotional trauma • Help with career transition issues • Provide comfort for family • Provide optimism • Reaffirm relationship	• Income needs • Managing settlement • Tax implications • Inventory of assets • Disposal of assets
Inheritance	• Understanding the emotional attachments that may come with the money • Providing rational advice or being the 'voice of reason' • Providing support and information on life changing opportunities • Helping other family members deal with new situation	• Financial planning education • Asset management • Asset disposal • Income changes • Lifestyle changes • Tax implications

Financial windfall	<ul><li>Understanding the emotional side of the windfall</li><li>Voice of reason and caution</li><li>Provide counsel for other family members</li><li>Take a financial education approach</li><li>Refer to other professionals if need be</li><li>Life Planning information</li><li>Providing support and information on life changing opportunities</li></ul>	<ul><li>Tax implications</li><li>Asset management</li><li>Spending changes</li><li>Income changes</li><li>Changes in employment situation</li><li>Lifestyle changes</li></ul>

The Life-First Advisor starts with the life transition and then wraps the solution around it. An advisor might ask, for example: "Bill, what are some of the implications of your retirement if you aren't able to work at your present job?" The discussion that follows might include the need for a critical illness policy, a more conservative investment approach, increased savings or additional life insurance.

Most financial planning issues are related to these life events and the advisor should continually try to create this association in the mind of the client. Consider these differences in approach between a Life-First Advisor and a typical financial advisor:

Two Different Approaches

Type of financial solution	Normal approach is to talk about	Life Transition approach is to focus on
Investment management	• Performance • Investment manager • Asset allocation • Risk tolerance • Tax issues • Fees • Investment type • Downside risk • Beta, efficient frontier	• Building a nest egg • Providing independence and flexibility when things change • Creating a legacy • Providing comfort through life changes • Providing income to finance lifestyle • Looking after loved ones
Insurance	• Monthly premium • Insurance benefit • Term vs whole life • Protect family or business • Disability • Business succession	• Protecting lifestyle at all stages • Creating a legacy • Protecting family • Creating income • Providing comfort in times of crisis
Estate planning	• Tax consequences • Planned giving • Distribution of assets • Reorganization of affairs • Wills, trusts	• Creating legacy • Helping family • Benevolence
Tax planning	• After-tax income • Deferral • Investment tax treatment • Trust accounts • Income splitting • Tax credits	• Creating legacy • Helping family • Benevolence • Increase lifestyle money

These are by no means the only considerations. And we're not saying an advisor would *never* talk about the issues covered in the traditional approach. The difference is the advisor only talks about these issues if he or she absolutely has to, and only in explaining how the life transition issues would be bridged.

An integrated strategy

The Life-First Approach creates an opportunity for the advisor to talk about an integrated approach to planning for the future, rather than a product-specific one.

The advisor doesn't bring up a specific product recommendation in the discussion. Instead, she converses with the client on all of the possible ramifications of the life change and then uses key points the client identifies as the basis for the financial solution to be recommended at the next meeting. Contrast this with the traditional 'I have a product, let me show you why you have a need' approach.

Life transitions aren't always apparent to the client, nor are they always assigned the importance they may deserve. A key role for the financial advisor is to be not just a catalyst who gets the client thinking but also an educator.

You can increase your value to the client by ensuring they are aware of all of the potential life transition issues. What life-changing events should the client be aware of? Are there things that could happen in the client's life that would be less of a concern if there were some pre-planning?

Think about time frames and gain an understanding of where the client sees potential issues or has concerns.

Of course, not all life transitions have negative consequences. Are there opportunities associated with a transition that the client could take advantage of by planning ahead?

Life so far

You can tell a lot about your client's ability to handle life transitions by bringing the conversation around to previous life changes. You might ask:

- How did they feel when they first had kids or grandkids?
- What kind of experiences have they had with changes at work?
- How did they adapt when their children left home and they became 'empty nesters'?
- How did they handle retirement?
- Have they had a major health challenge and did that change their outlook on life?

Again, these are topics that should be brought up in conversation in a way that doesn't confront. You wouldn't want to ask personal questions of someone you don't yet know very well, or who doesn't know you. That's where the 'art' of the conversation comes in – finding the appropriate time for such questions.

The bottom line is that you want to uncover as much information as you can in a way that feels natural for the client but also moves you towards a better understanding.

Specializing in Life Transitions

A growing number of advisors are using their approach to life transitions as a marketing tool for their practice. Specializing in transitions such as divorce, retirement lifestyle, 50-plus issues and career transition establishes a niche for them. This can be particularly important for securing professional referrals.

The Institute for Divorce Financial Analysts (www.institutedfa.com) conducts a four-day intensive course in the United States and Canada for advisors who wish to specialize in this area. To date, there are over 2000 Divorce Financial Analysts in the US and roughly 200 in Canada.

Most advisors with this designation use it to augment their current practice rather than as an actual identity for their service offering. "This is a very specialized market", one advisor said. "I make use of it for those clients who require specialized advice, but I haven't taken it to the level of becoming known as a 'divorce specialist'".

However, some advisors are using divorce transition planning as a branding tool. For example, one advisor focuses on how she can work with lawyers and accountants to help clients structure a financial plan during and after divorce.

This advisor sees her role as a financial professional as providing support during the settlement negotiations. More specifically, she aims to:

- Provide unbiased presentations of financial information and projections.

- Define and explain asset values, properties and tax implications.

- Develop realistic budgets that accurately portray future needs.

- Help clients focus on needs and values.

- Show long-term consequences of various settlement options.

- Provide a transition plan that focuses on the post-settlement period, with the goal of encouraging a sense of financial confidence and well-being.

"I always work with other professionals", she said. "I've taken the time to understand fully the implications that divorce or separation can have on the financial planning process, and I can be an important information source for other professionals, along with my clients and prospects".

Another example of using the transition approach as a marketing vehicle is the advisor who focuses on becoming an 'elder planning specialist'. There are many courses available to help people, including advisors, understand the social, health and emotional issues that seniors face. They cover topics such as:

- Bereavement and funeral planning

- Medicare and health care

- The social aspects of aging

- Long-term care, housing options and caregiving

- The aging process

- Communicating and marketing to 50-plus consumers

- Retirement lifestyle planning issues

- Ethics when working with seniors

Such courses help advisors understand and empathize with a maturing clientele. Well-informed advisors are able to conduct better conversations with clients, offer more relevant education programs and access experts in the community who can help clients with issues beyond the scope of a Life-First Advisor.

The Life-First Advisor ...

- Makes conversations about potential transitions part of their client discovery process
- Provides clients with education programs and information on life transition issues
- Educates themselves on specific life transitions so they understand both the financial and non-financial considerations

4 | Defining Your Value

- **Clients must understand that you do something different**
- **A value proposition should help your client understand intellectually and emotionally what you do for them**
- **The value proposition of a Life-First Advisor centers on three things: Clarity, Insight and Partnership**
- **Sincerity will always trump salesmanship**

You get into an elevator and meet someone who works in your building. It's just the two of you and you're traveling to the top of the building. The person smiles and asks, "So, what do you do for a living?"

Your first inclination is to answer, "I'm a financial advisor". But you stop because you think there may be an opportunity here to develop a new client. You know you only have a short time to tell this person what it is you do.

Your mind starts to race. "What is it that I do that this person would be interested in? How can I indicate I have something they need that would cause them to want to deal with me? What can I say that isn't going to make me sound like every other financial advisor or salesperson they've met?"

You kick yourself because you've been asked the same question hundreds of times and yet each time you have to think about it. As the elevator stops and the doors open, you reach into your pocket, pull out a business card and say, "I'm a financial advisor".

What's your value proposition?

Many advisors have a value proposition that focuses on the services they offer, what nice people they are or how trustworthy they are. These statements can fail to resonate because they tend to sound the same.

Think of your value proposition as a differentiation and branding statement. It should speak to a client in a way that makes them think, "I really need that" or "that's really different to what I'm getting now!"

You need to describe what you do in terms of what the client finds valuable. Your statement should be short, memorable, repeatable and say what you will do *for them* rather than just what you do.

Above the line

We've introduced the concept of 'above the line' and 'below the line'. These are useful ideas when you think about your value proposition, or how to explain what you do.

Remember, when you work above the line your focus is on people. When you work below the line your focus is on money, financial planning and investment management.

'Above the Line' and 'Below the Line'

This is WHY
you do it!

"PEOPLE"

This is WHAT & HOW
you do it!

"MONEY"

There's nothing wrong with working below the line. In fact, you couldn't do your job if you didn't go there. However, focusing on planning strategies isn't actually what you do – it supports what you *really* do. You do these things *because* you want to help clients achieve their life goals – the *why* part of the equation.

Noted advisor educator Bill Bachrach counselled in his book on values-based selling that "it is not what money is but what money does that is important!"[10]

Rather than focusing on delivering value through investment management, for example, the Life-First value proposition addresses how the advisor can meet a client's 'intrinsic' needs.

Intrinsic needs

'Intrinsic' refers to those internal motivators or needs we all have that make us feel better or give us satisfaction.

Remember Maslow and his hierarchy of needs? His pyramid was a description of intrinsic human needs that must be satisfied. His contention was that unsatisfied needs motivate us to take action.[11]

Looking at the value a wealth advisor brings to a client, the question to ask yourself is: What needs do they have that you meet?

Most advisors believe clients need things like investment management, tax planning and financial planning, and they define their value to the client in those terms. A sample of common value propositions used by advisors illustrates this:

"I help people make smart decisions about their money".

"I provide investment management advice with a difference".

"We are full-service wealth advisors who help you build financial plans".

"We help you reach your financial dreams and goals with an effective financial strategy".

---

[10] Bachrach, Bill, *Values-Based Selling*, 2001
[11] Maslow, Abraham, *A Theory of Human Motivation*, 1943

These don't actually describe what these advisors do to meet intrinsic needs, or how they do it. Differentiating between what, how and why is extremely important in marketing.

Later, we'll talk about how a good coach works with a person's internal thoughts, rather than providing them with external motivation. Simply put, you want to create pathways in the client's brain that change the way they view things.

A value proposition should help your client understand intellectually and emotionally what you do for them. If you tell them you'll build their wealth or provide them with a plan for retirement, you're relating to them on the basis of their money. If you express your value in terms of how you can make them feel better, your relationship is about them *as a person*.

What does a client need to get from your value proposition? Most would like an understanding of why they would want to work with you, or continue to work with you. If you consider their perspective, you'll position yourself as someone who can make their lives better because of the work you do.

Intrinsic needs come from our emotional center. Advisors can meet clients' intrinsic needs by:

- Helping them sort the sheer mass of information they are exposed to.
- Helping them understand what they need to plan for.
- Helping them clarify their vision.
- Coaching and mentoring them to help them stay on track.
- Providing perspective, experience and understanding.
- Helping them create and stick to the strategies needed to reach their goals.
- Educating them and helping them deal with their fears and biases.

As a Life-First Advisor your 'above-the-line' value rests in:

- Helping and protecting their families.
- Helping them enjoy and protect their lifestyle.
- Planning ahead for the expected and the unexpected.
- Creating a sense of financial comfort so they can sleep at night.
- Building a legacy.

These five elements are all 'right-brain' descriptors of the planning process and replace things like investment management, tax planning and financial planning.

As you look at these five aspects of the wealth, retirement or investment planning you do, think in these terms: "If I do these things properly for a client, I will meet their emotional, intrinsic needs".

Three things you do 'above the line'

Now that you understand the difference between what you do, how you do it and why you do it, we have a challenge: We want you to name three things you do for clients to meet their intrinsic needs – three things that could form the foundation of your value proposition.

By the way, communications experts tell us 'three' is the optimum number of points to make in a value proposition. Having one or two is not enough to make a strong point. Beyond three you're listing more things than most clients will remember. Use the 'power of three' to help clients remember what you say.

What I do above the line

1. _____

2. _____

3. _____

As you think about these three things, ask yourself: "What do I do for my clients that they find valuable that they can't get from anyone else?" You might say, "Wait a minute, my clients can get all of these things from other advisors!" While you might be right, what's the *one* thing they can't get elsewhere? The answer is *you* and the way you deliver these three things.

That's your answer any time somebody pushes back on your value proposition by saying their current advisor already does these things. For a start, most other advisors would never express their value proposition in the way we're proposing, and even if they did they could never deliver the three values in the way you will deliver them.

A simple way to lay it out

Many advisors have struggled with their value proposition over the years and a surprisingly large number either don't use it in their marketing or can't articulate it when asked.

As an industry, we're making this much more complicated than it needs to be. There are so many different approaches out there that many advisors have given up, unable to settle on one that makes sense for their practice.

But it's simple, really. A value proposition should be a straightforward explanation of what you do, defined in terms of why a client would care.

Your value proposition should have three parts. Address these questions when creating yours:

What do you do for the client? Thinking about the work you do in your day-to-day interaction with clients, how would you describe the main activity that benefits the client? Think in terms of the particular way you work with clients to make them feel better.

What expertise do you have that gives you the right to advise your client? This is your opportunity to showcase things such as your experience and expertise, and the team that works with you.

How do you work with your clients? Outline how you work in 'partnership' with clients.

When you describe what you do as a Life-First Advisor, focus on the things that set your approach apart. That means staying away from phrases like:

"I'm going to help you achieve your dreams".
"We provide you with peace of mind".
"We give you financial security".

Many advisors say they do these things, and they have rendered such phrases trite and unremarkable. Clients respond more to the things you do for them on a day-to-day basis than the 'pie in the sky' deliverables many advisors offer.

We've talked about the intrinsic needs clients have, the things they get from you every time they interact with you, the things that define your working/coaching relationship. This is where your real value to the client comes from.

For a Life-First Advisor, the value proposition comes down to clarity, insight and partnership.

You provide Clarity

There's an adage that says people 'don't know what they don't know'. There are so many things clients simply don't understand: What do they need to plan for? What should they be afraid of? What shouldn't they fear?

These sorts of emotional concerns surface when they read or watch the news – in fact, the media is so full of advice on what they should or shouldn't be doing that they need help to make sense of it all.

You provide your clients with clarity all the time but often take this part of your advisor role for granted. It's one of the most important things an advisor does and it should be part of every value proposition.

Providing clarity takes a number of forms for the Life-First Advisor:

- Your discovery process provides clients with a new way of thinking about their life and their money

- Your approach to investment management is disciplined and structured and doesn't try to control things you can't control, such as markets and stock prices

- Your client education program focuses on the issues that affect their lives and may have a financial impact

- You have an ongoing relationship with your client that reflects the life changes they experience

You provide Insight

Your clients also look to you to provide them with perspective, based on your education and experience and with the support of your firm and wider team of experts.

We all value experience and have great interest in what others have done in similar circumstances to our own. Your clients expect you to provide them with that insight as they think about the future.

While this might also be described as 'clarity', using insight as the second value you provide to your clients allows you to expand on the resources you can tap into within your team. This supports in more detail your right to provide counsel.

Insight is also about the understanding you have of the unique needs of your client. Share your personalized approach to understanding your client, and the way you conduct discovery, as you differentiate yourself.

You provide Partnership

The role of the advisor has changed considerably over the years. In the past, most advisors were facilitators, charging for services based on transactions.

Advisors were also the main source of information for most clients. They provided education, often with the goal of generating business. In fact, financial planning became a 'bait-and-switch' strategy to generate more transactions.

Today's client is looking for someone to work with on an ongoing basis. Transaction business is disappearing and compensation structures have been transformed. The value of the advisor now rests in the working relationship they build with the client.

Psychologists tell us we're more likely to take action if we enjoy a close relationship with the person advising us. Advisors understand the importance of rapport and relationship building in developing a successful practice.

As your client's partner, you move from the old 'teacher-student' dynamic and place yourself in the role of a key, trusted advisor.

Becoming the 'primary advisor'

The Life-First Advisor seeks to become their client's *primary* advisor by positioning their value in terms of being the one person who sees the whole picture, who can provide that clarity, insight and partnership.

Many advisors aspire to this role but define their value 'below the line', pointing to their financial expertise and promoting concepts such as the Family Office or personal 'Chief Financial Officer'.

But the primary advisor also needs people expertise and a wider perspective.

The primary advisor actively promotes their role as a team leader for other relationships gathered by the client. A good analogy is that the primary advisor is like a medical doctor in general practice who works with specialists to help a patient.

Guard against the 'I got a guy' approach to developing your wider team, though, if you truly want to be thought of as the primary advisor. Some advisors won't talk about basic planning issues because they have neither the expertise nor the licensing to do so. That's understandable but it also means someone else can come in and establish primary advisor positioning.

Rather than pretending that those other financial planning issues don't exist, focus your discussions on the five key areas we outlined earlier:

- Helping and protecting a client's family
- Helping them enjoy and protect their lifestyle
- Planning ahead for the expected and the unexpected
- Creating a sense of financial comfort so they can sleep at night
- Building a legacy

From a business standpoint, studies suggest that as your client's key, trusted advisor you'll control more assets, generate more fees, attract more referrals and retain more clients with such a positioning.

According to a 2013 study by the Oechsli Institute, 84 percent of affluent clients considered their financial advisor to be their primary *financial* professional. However, it also found that those clients who viewed their advisor as a 'primary financial advisor' only felt comfortable entrusting 30 percent of their assets to that individual.[12]

---

[12] Oechsli, Matt: Understanding the affluent investor, 2013

We know that those advisors who establish a relationship transcending money, who take an 'above the line' approach, can become a key trusted advisor, not just a key trusted *financial* advisor.

The key trusted advisor can always fulfil functions below the line. However, it is virtually impossible for someone who works only below the line to become the primary advisor.

Communicating your value proposition

The Life-First Advisor feels they have something of value beyond selling a product or service. They look for every opportunity to explain what they do in a way that doesn't impose on or confront the listener.

Communicating a value proposition is very much a matter of personal style. It has to be in your own words and you have to believe in what you say. It can't sound too 'sales-y' and it has to be of interest to the listener.

Experience has shown that many advisors are insecure when it comes to proclaiming what they do. "I could never do an elevator speech", said one advisor. "I wouldn't want the person to turn off as soon as I opened my mouth!"

One of the most important communications principles is that an audience focuses first on how something is said rather than on the words themselves. The leap of faith that advisors have to take when they explain their value proposition is that sincerity will always win out.

So, whenever someone asks what you do, explain things in simple terms while showing your sincerity and demonstrating your value.

Potential client: *Hi John, I haven't seen you for a while. What are you doing now?*

Life-First Advisor: *Well, my business card says I'm a wealth advisor, but let me explain what that really means. I work with clients to provide them with clarity around the things they need to plan for financially. I provide them with insight, based on my own experience and working with a team of experts, and having an understanding of* *their personal situation. And I provide them with partnership as they move through the stages of their lives, helping them update their plans for the future. That's what I do as a professional financial advisor.*

Should you have different value propositions depending on your audience?

No. You should have the same value proposition. But you can augment it with a phrase like: "Here are the three things I provide for this market". We used Clarity, Insight and Partnership above for a private client. You could use the same words to describe how you work with a corporate client or center of influence:

Corporate client: *Tell me why you're different to other advisors.*

Life-First Advisor: *What makes me different is the way I provide clients with three key things. First, I work with corporate clients to help them clarify the issues they need to plan for when it comes to employee benefit programs, education and options for employees. Second, I provide companies with my insight and expertise on the opportunities available to them, and the issues they may not have thought about – always based on the deep understanding I have of the company. Finally, I work as a partner with my corporate clients to ensure their plans always reflect the realities for both the company and its employees.*

After you've settled on your value proposition, practice it as much as possible so the words are yours and the sincerity comes through. Remember, you have to own it.

You'll find that it will flow and you won't even think about whether to use it or not. You'll always be communicating your value to people who will actually be interested in what you have to say.

The Life-First Advisor's value proposition differs from that of most other advisors. Be ready to tell people what you really do and the real value you provide by meeting both their financial and emotional needs.

A video script

A number of advisors have added video to their websites to help them explain to clients in right-brain terms what they do.
Here's one example of a script:

Let me ask you two questions: One, what do you expect your financial advisor to do for you? Two, what do you value most about your financial advisor?

My name is Alan Mitchell and I'm a Certified Financial Planner with clients in the Melbourne area. When I meet with people who may require the help of a professional advisor I'm often struck by their answers.

Most people have expectations of their advisors that are tied to performance of markets or things that are beyond the control of any human being. They also believe my value to them surrounds the advice that I provide around money or investments.

My clients value three things from the relationship that I have with them. In the course of applying these to financial issues that they may face I've been able to make a positive impact on their lives and the lives of their family.

First, I help my clients clarify the key planning issues they need to think about both today and tomorrow. Much of our discussion focuses on life needs, concerns and goals – all of which will drive the plan we create together.

Second, I provide them with the insight and perspective that comes from my own business perspective. Insight doesn't just come from what I know, but what I know about them.

Finally, I work as a partner with my client. As time passes and life changes, we're able to adjust the plans and strategies to better reflect your situation. If there's anything in my client's life that has a financial element to it, I want them to be comfortable enough to make me one of the first calls they make!

In short, my value to my clients comes from our mutual understanding of their life issues. What sets me apart is that my client is a person and not a portfolio or a bank account. Investment management or financial planning isn't what I do but how I do it!

If that's the kind of advisor you've been looking for, I'd love the opportunity to talk further to see how you can benefit from working together.

The Life-First Advisor ...

- Creates a value proposition that is 'above the line'
- Focuses on how the advisor and client work together in a partnership
- Ensures clients understand the advisor's value proposition
- Applies the value proposition to aspects such as discovery and marketing

5 | The Advisor as Coach

- **The Life-First Advisor is more than an advisor – they are a coach**
- **Coaches are catalysts, helping clients recognize issues for themselves**
- **In the future, advisors will be paid for their ability to partner with their clients rather than just working with their money**

Everyone has a 'coach' they remember, someone who believed in them and helped them focus. In sharing their experience, that person changed our thinking and helped us clarify what we wanted to achieve, while giving us the skills to get there.

What separates the Life-First Advisor from other advisors is the role they play as a coach, helping clients understand both the short-term and long-term issues that require a financial planning strategy, and keeping them on track.

Some advisors now consider themselves 'life coaches' and have taken coaching certification to fulfil this role. Their approach is to use behavioral finance principles to ensure clients stick to the advice they receive and shut out distracting external influences such as media 'noise'.

What do coaches do?

"Interaction with a fellow human being, especially one who can understand what you're going through and direct your awareness to the solutions you can use, is a powerful approach to self-help."

— Haider Al-Mosawi, thought leader

As your role in the client's life evolves, you become more of a mentor, educator and coach than purely advisor. While there's nothing wrong with traditional services such as creating a financial plan, helping clients grow their wealth and steering them to make smart decisions about their money, these all relate to the client's financial situation. Your role in this scenario is to provide external motivation. In fact, your true client is not the person but the portfolio, the bank book or the financial plan.

A better approach is to help your client become internally motivated, thinking about what you say and then applying it to their own situation. In this role, you help the client develop a thinking pattern that will empower, motivate and reinforce.

If you take on a coaching role, you are forcing the client to view you in different terms. You are encouraging them to *think* not just to act. You are also helping them organize their thoughts by discovering their motivators, those 'hot buttons' that are the foundation of conscious or deliberate action.

The four tenets of coaching

If this chart looks familiar, reread the previous chapter on what your value proposition should be! By taking these four tenets of coaching and applying them to the value you present to your client, you redefine your role from financial advisor to coach.

Think of how in the world of sport a coach uses past insight to work with an athlete to clarify the skills they need to master. In the partnership role, the coach works with the athlete to hone the skills through repetition and feedback. This keeps the athlete accountable and the process engenders self-discovery.

Brain science and coaching

Clients are focused either internally or externally. Simply put, their motivations come primarily from within or are a result of external stimulus.

Coaching works because it helps clients organize their thoughts by changing awareness, creating focus, promoting skill building and offering ongoing support.

As an advisor, you can help clients change their perspective, concentrate on the key issues and then create an ongoing relationship with them to incorporate the right habits into a financial plan.

While a key role of an advisor is to ensure clients understand what's important to them and to stay focused on those issues, this is easier said than done. For one thing, clients don't always know what their priorities are and, in any case, are pulled to and fro by the media, their own lack of focus or a lack of interest.

Brain science research suggests self-directed goals can actually change the way the brain works. The theory is that when we take a problem or task and 'think it through', we can rewire our brains and create new thought pathways. Psychologists call this 'fluid intelligence', because we are working through issues and problems internally rather than making decisions based purely on external advice.

When your clients are thinking about the important issues that drive their financial decisions, they need a perspective they find relevant.

That is why advisors taking a life-based approach are more successful in helping the client internalize.

Coaching your client's brain

Coaching has these three impacts on clients' ability to focus:

Attention Density – This refers to your client's ability to sort out many different ideas and concentrate on the message you want them to internalize. A new thought comes into our heads every 10 seconds or so – more often if there is a competing external source. While coaching is also an external source, it provides structure and a bulwark against extraneous ideas.

Homeostasis – Our natural inclination is to change focus constantly. Homeostasis refers to an ability to stay the course and not be distracted. Coaching reinforces the message and keeps the client's eye on the goal.

Neuroplasticity – We all have differing capacities to accept new information and to use fluid thinking, and our ability reduces as we age. Coaching increases neuroplasticity by helping the client organize thoughts and think about the issues that are important.

The importance of self-discovery

Coaches are catalysts in that they understand that the more they can help clients recognize issues for themselves, the more effective the clients will be in mastering the skills needed to improve.

Everyone has a way of looking at the world. Many clients have preconceived notions about how to invest, about what financial planning is and about how to plan for retirement.

This is their paradigm, their 'way of thinking'. A coach can change that paradigm by getting them to internalize a fresh view so they harness the power of their own brain and gain clarity.

Psychologist Tim Ursiny says "people will not easily change their minds if they come to a conclusion through self-discovery."[13] It's better to help clients discover a new perspective themselves because that way they're more likely to stick with the plan.

Your clients' coachable goals

An internal goal that requires your client to grow or improve as a person in order to achieve it is called a coachable goal. This is in contrast to traditional goals that involve an external achievement or life destination.

For instance, we might think a weight loss program or self-improvement course can help us become 'better people'. The challenge in setting and reaching these types of goals is they normally require much more than simply stating a 'New Year's Resolution'. It's simple to make wishes. Achieving a goal is easier with a coach to keep you on track.

Clients have two kinds of goals. Extrinsic goals are normally associated with, say, wealth, career and travel, while intrinsic goals are usually associated with personal development and life satisfaction. Most financial advisors focus clients on the former.

While we all need extrinsic goals or bucket lists to stay motivated, where we gain most satisfaction is in meeting intrinsic goals. Reaching intrinsic goals has been directly related to increased health and wellbeing.

In addition, the more we internalize and identify with a goal by understanding the value behind it, or even simply the importance of the task, the more likely we are to act autonomously. This is where the advisor as coach can help. The client is self-actualizing but with the help and mentoring of the advisor.

Goals are aspirational, though the concept of reaching a goal is finite. A better approach to the goal conversation is to talk about 'possibilities' rather than just reaching a finish line. Get the client to always think about what could happen that he or she can control or

---

[13] Ursiny, Tim, *Coaching the Sale*, 2006

influence with your coaching.

Personal coaching isn't therapy, by the way. If you look at what coaches actually do you'll find you already do many of the same things. The Life-First Advisor simply formalizes the process by ensuring clients recognize the advisor's coaching role.

Are you a coach already?

Coaches help clients set personal goals and then focus them on the strategy needed to get there. Isn't that what you already do?

Your clients put you in the position of challenging their decisions or acting as a sounding board. In fact, if you haven't made it safe for your client to look to you as a personal coach your communication may only be at the most superficial level.

As part of the financial planning process you clarify the client's current situation and ensure they understand exactly where they are. This includes helping them understand their 'inner selves', their behavioral biases and their needs, concerns and opportunities.

As a coach, you'll use your insight and experience to help clients think about the role money plays in their future. A Life-First Advisor enhances this by gaining a sound understanding of the client through the discovery process.

The Life-First Advisor helps the client become an effective planner and critical thinker when it comes to money, just as a sports coach keeps the athlete focused and adaptive to change.

However, here's where the 'disconnect' occurs between what a personal coach does and how many financial advisors view this kind of interaction:

- Personal coaches facilitate, motivate, educate, support and challenge their clients to build and attain their goals. Most financial advisors assume clients can do this for themselves

- Financial advisors assume people know how to set goals and that all of their clients have a clear view and understanding of their future

- While some advisors educate themselves on the process of becoming a personal coach, many others don't

Despite these variances, most advisors with trusting clients are in a coaching role whether they recognize it or not.

In thinking about this distinction, ask yourself how often a client has confided in you about an issue that is not strictly financial in nature? They'll only do so if they view you as a critical part of their decision-making.

Five keys to becoming a coach

- Your clients must view you as a source of information and a resource on life planning issues (though not necessarily an expert, like a psychologist)

- You must show you relate financial planning to life planning

- You must be a good listener, questioner, challenger and facilitator

- You must be prepared to 'get personal'. Insist you can't offer effective financial planning unless you understand relevant elements of their life plan

- Your clients have to feel you are a true partner and mentor

The language of coaching

Words matter, especially when you're coaching someone. As an advisor you can use 'coaching language' to help clients see you in a different way. If you act as a partner, your discussion becomes more of a conversation than an inquisition. You want to make the client feel comfortable and to create the 'we' space that will help them open up and think about what you're saying.

To help clients create an internal dialogue, use pictures and other strategies that assist them in organizing their thoughts and take the discussion into the right brain. In a later chapter, we show how the Life-First Discovery process is designed to accomplish this.

Closed-ended questions (ones that can be answered 'yes' or 'no') are fine so long as follow-up questions get the client to expand. A coach is less interested in answers to questions that start with 'can', 'are', 'do' and 'will' as they are in questions that start with 'what' and 'how'.

Coaching language is clear and direct in order to elicit clear and direct answers. For example:

- 'Do' instead of 'try'.
- 'Will' instead of 'might'.
- 'Want' instead of 'need'.
- 'Must' instead of 'could'.

The elements of a good conversation

When looking at brain science we talked about the music of a conversation and how to resonate with your client by using mirroring. Your interaction should feel more like an informal conversation than an inquisition.

In fact, one of the lost arts in our business is the ability to just talk to people. While most advisors jump right to the discovery process, for the intuitive advisor the conversation is the discovery process.

To make effective use of conversation, the following things have to happen:

- The conversation has to be a 'two-way street.' In other words, the advisor has to be able to share personal information with the client. For example, a prospect's comment that they have a 10-year-old grandchild could be met with the advisor's comment, *"I have two children who are 10 and 12. They sure are a delight at that age!"*

- A prospective client has to feel comfortable enough to open up emotionally. In an initial interview that means getting them talking about their life issues. That discussion provides context for any financial plan.

- The client must feel the conversation has a purpose, so open the discussion with something like: *"Mrs Jones, bear with me for a few minutes because I'd like to get to know you a little better."*

- Body language, eye contact and facial expression must convey you are interested and care about what the client or prospect has to say.

- 'Active listening' phrases should encourage the client to expand on what they've just said. (*"Tell me what you mean by that..."* or *"Can you give me more detail?"*)

When discussions get rocky, coaches make use of the 'meta conversation' – a conversation about the conversation. The aim is to get the client to focus on why the conversation is causing them some difficulty.

Throughout, you must remain an intuitive listener. That means not only paying attention to what clients say but also what they don't say. Spotting such omissions requires 'empathic listening', or seeing the world through their eyes.

This is like conversational first aid. You help clients uncover implicit needs and make them explicit. Your interventions at this point can be quite simple, with questions such as "Did you know...?" or "Have you thought about...?"

The result is the client views money issues through a different prism, because the structure becomes life-based or internal rather than finance-based or external.

The cost of not using this approach is the conversation becomes guarded and never gets beyond the mechanics of money. Trust doesn't develop and the dialogue never reaches a point where the underlying issues are revealed.

Empathic listening

Here are some conversational tools that empathic listeners use to move the conversation forward and to make the client feel safe enough to share:

Repeat what you've heard. This shows the client you're making every effort to understand. Repeating is an active listening technique but is less effective if you don't use what you've heard to help the client explore the issue in more depth. For example:

Client: *I'm worried about my portfolio and all the uncertainty around.*
Advisor: *So you're worried about your portfolio. Why don't we talk about that? Help me to understand what concerns you.*

Other phrases to use are:

- "I'm going to repeat what you just said to make sure I heard you..."

- "Let me repeat what I heard..."

This allows you to use the client's statement as a point of departure that opens up a new discussion topic.

Rephrase what you've heard. This is often used to create understanding. You are putting the client's words in your own terms and then getting the client to accept the rephrased version. For example:

Client: *I haven't thought much about putting together a long-term plan for my business. Things change so quickly that it just makes no sense.*

Advisor: *So what you are saying is that you think having a long-term business transition plan is unnecessary?*

Other phrases to use are:

- "So what that really means to you is ... (advisor's own words).
- "So if I hear you correctly, you are saying ... "

This can be a powerful technique, if done well, because it gives clients a different perspective. It also helps you to get to the real issues or implicit needs the client may not have thought about.

Reflect emotion. Acknowledging the client's feelings about an issue, either by commiserating or sharing similar emotion, can be powerful if used in moderation. It helps establish common ground. For example:

Client: *Thinking about retirement, I get really worried about whether I've considered everything that's going to be important to me then.*
Advisor: *I know what you mean. I often have the same worries. There's always something that blindsides you – and this is my profession!*

If you use the 'I feel your pain' approach honestly you are communicating at both a conscious and subconscious level, establishing that you really do understand how the client is feeling.

The ideal approach is to rephrase what the client has said, get them to acknowledge your rephrasing and then reflect your emotion around the rephrased statement as the capstone to the discussion point.

Traps to avoid

Many advisors tend to examine a client's answers in the context of their own paradigms. This is called the 'autobiographical filter' and it's the biggest impediment to empathic listening. You can't really understand what a client is saying if you don't put yourself in their shoes.

Some of the most common ways advisors project their views with clients are:

Being too ready to show the client how wrong they are. While you have a teaching role, this can stop the client from sharing. This response becomes judgmental as the advisor uses what the client is reflecting to demonstrate capability. For example:

Client: *The markets are far too risky to invest in right now – I'm uncomfortable.*

Advisor: *But the markets aren't risky if you take a long-term view. Let me show you this Morningstar chart with the performance of stocks, bonds, bills and inflation since 1926 to show you that you shouldn't be concerned.*

Using your own experience as a frame of reference. This is when you propose a solution that would fit you but not necessarily the client. It's one thing to say you understand, but jumping to a solution based on how you would handle it may miss the mark entirely. For example:

Client: *All equity investments are risky because you could lose your money.*

Advisor: *But savvy investors understand that you have to take risks in order to generate returns.*

The client's concern may have nothing to do with the mathematics of market performance but be about their concern with volatility. The advisor missed an opportunity to acknowledge what the client said and to understand what was actually behind it.

10 steps to adding a 'coaching' flavor to your business

1. Position yourself as a coach from the outset. Advisors *tell* clients. Coaches *ask* them.

2. Use the discovery process to help the client understand the key life issues that drive their financial decisions.

3. Take seriously your role as an educator to encourage your client to draw their own conclusions.

4. Run education programs that focus on life issues or the relationship between life and money. The client gains a fresh perspective on what you do.

5. Hone your skills as a conversationalist, including being a good listener and practicing empathic listening.

6. Use the coaching questions: 'Did you know...?' and 'Have you thought about...?'

7. Provide a basic structure on how to think about life and money and use that as the foundation for your coaching conversation.

8. Employ a meta-conversation whenever you sense the client is uncomfortable.

9. Clarify your client's life needs, concerns, opportunities and goals before moving to a financial discussion.

10. Take a coaching course through an organization like The International Coaching Federation or Coach University (available online).

The Life-First Advisor changes how the client thinks about planning, money and the role the advisor plays. In short, by positioning yourself as a coach you become the kind of advisor your client 'did not know they were looking for'.

The Life-First Advisor ...

- Understands the need to 'get personal'
- Is skilled in the art of conversation and an empathic listener
- Helps clients stay focused and on track
- Encourages clients to think, not just act

6 | Managing Client Relationships

- **The Life-First Advisor is an integral part of the client's life**

- **Being a 'partner' means having regular and consistent contact**

- **Channels can vary but personal contact wherever possible is key**

The client meeting is the major event in the financial planning process. It's also a critical element of your branding, the way you differentiate your practice and the way the client perceives the value you bring.

Obviously there are differences between a meeting with a long-established client and one with a new prospect. But in both you need conversational skills to make the client comfortable and to get into deeper issues that engage them.

These meetings have three goals. They should:

- Extend your brand and differentiate your practice

- Create a conversation that helps uncover emotional 'hot buttons'

- Reinforce your value in the client's mind

While the subject of 'money' and 'investment return' are going to come up, they should be in the context of the bigger Life-first picture.

In a prospect meeting or first meeting naturally you want to establish your particular approach as a differentiator. However, even in a service meeting or routine interaction you still need to accomplish these three goals.

Regular connections

Clients recognize your value in many ways if you give them the opportunity to do so. You want to stay 'top of mind' and reinforce the value you bring.

Unfortunately, many advisors fail to keep in regular touch and feel they're imposing by holding regular meetings. "My clients don't want to see me that much", is a typical response or, "As far as I'm concerned, if they only want to see me once a year I have to respect their wishes".

Matt Oechsli's study of affluent clients in 2013 found that 43 percent met with their advisor face-to-face once or twice a year. A further 25 percent had three or four meetings annually[14].

Life-First Advisors seek ways to get in front of the client as often as possible and reinforce their approach at every opportunity. This doesn't always have to involve a face-to-face meeting – though one a year is probably insufficient to keep up with a client's life changes and sustain trust. Social events, Skype or Facetime, Zoom etc. are examples that can fill the gap. You want to 'touch' your client as much as you can without being intrusive. All touches should reinforce your value of clarity, insight and partnership.

How frequent should contact be? The simple answer is as often as needed to create and maintain a positive emotional connection. Explain to your clients that regular contact is essential to you providing your best advice and support.

Reinforcing your brand through client contact

Client interaction is an opportunity to reinforce your brand. This could be as simple as the way your office looks, through to the design of handouts and the style of seminars and workshops you hold.

Your clients have to know what it is you do for them. Sometimes you have to find ways to remind them of the value you bring. That doesn't mean you keep hammering them with "I did this" or "look at the benefit

---

[14] Oechsli, Matt, The Oechsli Institute, 2013

you received from that", though. Here's how one advisor deals with it:

"Jack, I want you to remember that whenever we do anything from a financial planning perspective, we always try to tie it to a particular life planning issue you have."

Don't take for granted that your client always understands what you do. You need to reinforce your value proposition continually by the way you conduct your meetings.

Don't forget the oxytocin response

When we looked at brain science earlier, we talked about the oxytocin response and the need to have your clients 'like' you. In our business, 'out of sight, out of mind' is a danger to a long-term relationship. You want as many face-to-face or phone contacts as possible – without being intrusive – to remind your client why they like you!

The Life-first Advisor has a systematic approach to client contact that ensures the maximum number of touches possible. Your client segmentation will influence your contact schedule but remember that you, not the client, 'drive the bus' when it comes to how often to have contact. Regular contact is essential to maintaining your role as a coach and positioning yourself as the key trusted advisor.

The discovery process works best if client and advisor agree to regular review meetings. We recommend a quarterly review rather than a semi-annual or annual. We also believe the meeting should be face-to-face rather than on the phone. This helps the client make an emotional connection with the advisor – one that might be lost through an impersonal phone call.

Systemize your meeting approach

Here's an example of a set process for meetings:

- The client is always greeted by the receptionist or marketing assistant and offered a refreshment. The client's preference is noted for future use

- The assistant draws the client's attention to your firm's brochure

- The client sits for a maximum five minutes in a comfortable waiting area that is set up to tell the advisor's story through items such as pictures, community service plaques and life-transition information pieces

- The client is brought to the meeting room through the main part of the office, to subtly showcase the team that supports them

A consistent process at each meeting helps your client form an impression about what your practice stands for and who you are.

Meeting set-up

If the meeting is in your office, it should be held in a place that signals you take a different approach to everyone else. Small details matter.

- Focus on client comfort. As a desk creates a psychological barrier, use a round table so the client feels you're working alongside them. A non-threatening 'living room' layout invites conversation

- Instead of financial planning charts, hang pictures that showcase your values, your family, hobbies and aspirations. These signal you are a different type of advisor and provide talking points

- One advisor we know created a 'dream wall'. Each client is given a frame during their annual review to fill with pictures of the important elements of their lives. Above all the pictures on the dream wall are the words: 'These are the things in life that really matter'

- Every little thing from coffee cups to glasses to stationery offers a subtle comment on your practice. Hand the client a cup with a fund manager's logo on it and you'll undo a lot of the work that's gone into your Life-First branding

Next steps – a process

The Life-First approach is a four-step process that helps the client understand the real value of the financial plan – from vision to strategy to implementation to review.

The relationship involves a continuous re-evaluation of where they are in life and what changes or challenges they expect in the future.

Clients should come to understand that you will use the same approach every time.

Continuous re-evaluation

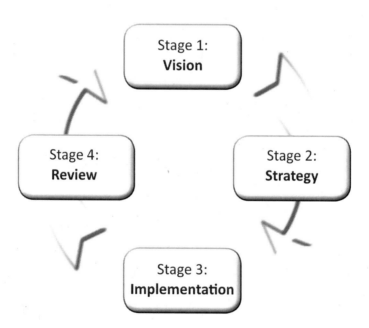

The Life-First Discovery process, which we cover more fully in the next chapter, fits into every kind of meeting you have with a client. Here's how you can incorporate it.

Meeting with a new prospect

The prospect will likely be interviewing you as much as you are trying to get to know them. For your part, the first task is to ensure they understand your approach, while making them feel comfortable about you.

Don't jump to solutions in the first meeting. Even if you're clear on what needs to be done, exercise patience and focus on a few small objectives:

- Provide written information about your firm
- Set the stage so the prospect understands your proposition
- Focus on the conversation map as the center of discussion

The goals of the prospect meeting are to:

- Give prospects a reason to come back for a full meeting
- Show prospects your approach is unique
- Make prospects feel the meeting was 'all about them'
- Assess whether there is a business fit

Normally, there is no pre-meeting work as the prospect is there to interview you. But you also want to gain some control as they assess you. At the outset, state your Life-First value proposition:

"George, we've been looking forward to exploring how we may be of value to you. We take a lot of pride in showing our clients we have a different approach than you might be used to. We want you to feel we'll use our knowledge and experience to provide you with information that benefits your life planning. Our goal is to help you with the financial implications of the life issues you encounter. You'll find our discussions will focus on what it is you want to accomplish and then together we'll make financial plans."

Whatever you say at the outset, focus on what the prospect can expect from you that will be beneficial and distinctive. Of course, you also must identify their expectations. Simply starting with, "Now George, how can I help you today?" isn't going to do it!

Pre-Discovery: Is there a business fit?

Don't take a prospect through the full Life-First Discovery process until you've assessed whether there is a fit between you.

Again, this depends on the prospect and whether you feel you can afford to spend substantial time on discovery before assessing whether to take it further.

Traditionally, your options are to ask the client to bring in financials or perhaps have them fill out an online questionnaire. The danger here is it suggests you're more interested in the money than in the client. An alternative is to ask these five questions:

"Tell me about your current financial situation". This gives you a quick impression of how prospects view their planning needs.

"What do you need an advisor to do for you?" This tells you about the prospect's previous experience with advisors.

"What factors are you worried will have a financial impact on you?" This helps you understand how the client views long-term planning.

"What do you worry most about when you think about your money?" This helps you understand risk tolerance and behavioral finance biases.

"Why did you come to us for help?" This provides a good overview of the client's expectations and how they learned about your firm.

While these questions won't reveal all the information you may ultimately need, they're a good starting point in assessing fit. Once you've decided to work with them, you move into the more formal Life-First Discovery process.

The key point is these questions should be up front because part of your value proposition is that you want to be the advisor the prospect 'didn't know they were looking for'.

Next, get a commitment to move forward. A great way to do this is to sum up the meeting by saying:

"Mrs Smith, I hope we've been able to show you that we can help you plan for the future through the approach we take. Based on our discussion today, are we the kind of firm you'd like to work with?" or

"Mr Jones, we've discussed a number of potential areas of concern for you and we've given you a sense of how we approach the financial planning process. Based on our meeting today, would you like to go forward with a more in-depth planning session?"

You want to focus on the Life-First Discovery process. Here's how an advisor might set up the approach:

"George, as I said at the outset, we try to take a more personal approach here. We've been successful with our clients because we get to understand a lot of their issues that may potentially need our help. In fact, we call our system the 'Life-First' financial advice process. We want you to get to know us so you feel comfortable, but we also want to get to know you better at the same time."

You want this first session to feel comfortable for the prospect. Remember, they're assessing you at the same time you're learning about them.

What not to do …

- Don't let the meeting go on past the point where either party is gaining benefit

- Don't rush into the planning discussion. Ideally, you shouldn't do it at all in this initial session. Tell the prospect you first want to fully understand what they are trying to accomplish

- Don't give the client anything to read that doesn't brand you as a Life-First Advisor

At the end of your session, you should have achieved the following:

- Your prospect understands you are a Life-First Advisor
- You have an understanding of potential 'hot' buttons to focus on later
- Your prospect feels comfortable with you and your approach

Meeting with an existing client

Many advisors who want to shift to the Life-First process ask how they should introduce the new approach to their existing clients. The answer is that you don't have to change absolutely everything. In fact, the shift to a Life-First approach is more a natural evolution of your process than a fundamental overhaul of what you do. Here's how one advisor introduced the approach:

"John, we've always taken the same approach to your financial plan but I want to add a new element from this point on. As my clients move through various stages of their work and their lives, we're asked to provide additional support in areas that we may not have talked about. Also, my company has a lot of resources that we haven't had to use up to this point, but we may in the future. For that reason, I'm going to ask you some questions that I may not have asked before, and we'll look at some areas of possible concern that we should be planning for."

Moving to discovery

Advisors are often torn about what information to ask the client to bring to the formal discovery meeting. Some want the full financial package, while others want to wait until the financial discovery session to review financial documents.

Whatever you choose, remember to set the client's financial information aside once you get it. The minute you pick up the package you're saying to the client you're more interested in the financial information than you are in them.

Four types of meeting

Pre-Meeting Package	• Establish brand and outline process	• Intro Letter describing process • Brochure	• Move to Planning meeting
Discovery or Clarity Meeting	• Establish brand • Build trust • Demonstrate capability by outlining the Life-First Process • Uncover 'hot' buttons through conversation • Collect financial information	• Expectations tool • Values Planning Map • Summary sheet • Other possible tools: • Life Planning software (if used) • Personal financial comfort assessment (verbally)	• Mail Pre-meeting package for meeting #2 (have them bring their financial information) • Assess meeting information • Review financial information • Formulate proposal • Arrange for proposal meeting
Strategy or Insight Meeting	• Reinforce brand • Make proposal based on assessment • Tie proposal to life goals and gain agreement	• Financial planning software (if used)	• Arrange for next update meeting • Update on upcoming value-added events
Regular progress or Partnership Meetings	• Reinforce brand • Update client info (structured conversation) • Update financial goals • Tie financial goals to life goals and gain agreement • Update life transition assessment • Assess client's life planning needs	• Expectations conversation • Values map • Life Planning software (if not used previously)	• Review financial and life transition update; make recommendations • Update client on upcoming workshops or value-added programs

Pre-meeting package

This is used when you first meet with a new client or when you meet with an established client and want to reinforce your transition to the Life-first approach. Use the package to provide the Life-First Tools and to lay out the methodology you use in your financial planning practice. Key elements of the package include:

Brochure or video on your practice to a client or new client. This is right-brain positioning establishing you as a Life-First Advisor. It's the most valuable marketing piece you have because it explains why your approach is different.

Initial letter to a new client. This outlines the details of the meeting as well as requests for additional information to bring to the meeting. The letter to a new client will be different than to an existing client (see samples at the end of this chapter).

A meeting agenda outline. This is used to outline the goals of the meeting. It can accompany the pre-meeting package, or it can be given in person at the time of booking the next meeting.

Most importantly, the presentation should illustrate the professional approach you take with all of your clients and differentiate you from your competition. Naturally, the information should be concise and written from the client's perspective. Phrase statements about your services in terms of benefits.

Finally, in putting the pre-meeting package together, ensure there is no attempt in the documents to 'sell' a product.

Goal-setting questionnaire

When you come to review your client's financial plan at your update meetings, pay attention to life planning areas.

The client questionnaire below poses some personal questions in areas including their health, their relationships and their personal and professional goals. You don't necessarily have to see their answers but you *do* want them to think about the financial consequences of their goals. You're in a position to help them with these.

This tool should become part of your methodology with as many clients as possible. It helps both you and the client relate money to life.

Annual Client Review – <u>Regular Progress Meeting</u>

To help us maintain your financial plan and understand the relationship between your money and your life goals, we'd like you to take a few minutes to consider your feelings on the following questions ...

1. The areas we want you to think about are:

	In the next year....?	In the next five years...?	In the next phase of my life?	Possible Financial implications
Purchases I want to make in the future				Finance major purchases Home and mortgage Investments to make Lifestyle 'toys' Upgrading or replacing present possessions Changes in net worth
Personal or professional achievements I want to reach				Self-improvement expenses Continuing education investment Changes in income or benefits Changes in net worth Tax obligations
Fulfilling activities I want to undertake				Financing major activities Ongoing availability of: Lifestyle money Special events money Debt management or service
Relationships I want to develop or strengthen				Gifts, bequests Charitable giving Assist parents Assist children Joint financial goals Investment in others Insurance
How I want to feel physically				Lifestyle pursuits Health and nutrition spending New activities Long- or short-term disability Critical illness Critical care Longevity

Things I want to learn				Education expenses Travel expenses Career changes Financial self-education Technology investment
Desired emotional well-being that will let me enjoy my life				Current and future income Health investment Disability insurance Career or income changes Charitable giving Investment choices
The questions of my life and my world that I want to understand				Self-education Travel expenses Career or lifestyle changes

2. What areas of your financial plan are of the most concern to you today?

Area of financial planning	Reason for concern?	Effect on life plan?	Possible course of action?

3. What are the major areas of your life and goals that have changed since we last met?

1	
2	
3	
4	
5	
6	

As a Life-First Advisor you want to be an integral part of your client's life, and as their partner you need to have regular and personal contact. The client meeting is the major event in the financial planning process and it's critical to get it right.

The Life-First advisor ...

- Stays in touch with clients so they are 'top of mind'
- Reinforces their brand via every interaction
- Takes a systematic approach

Pre-Meeting Letter to a new client

John Jones
123 My Street
Toronto, ON
M8X 2Y2

<first name> <last name>
<address>
<city>, <province>
<postal code>

Dear <first name>:

We look forward to learning more about how we can benefit you with our experience and expertise. We take a lot of pride in the way we work with clients and feel it sets us apart from the many financial advisors available to you.

The Life-First Approach to wealth management simply means we make every effort to learn as much as we can about the way your financial situation can positively impact your life and the lives of your family.

You will find everything we do with our clients relates financial planning to the much broader issues that affect their lives. You will also see the seminars we provide for our clients, the newsletter we write and the way we conduct our financial planning process all focus on helping you 'turn success into significance'.

We have enclosed a brief overview of our services, our team and our philosophy. We hope you will go through it as it will give you a good picture of the value our clients receive. We have also enclosed two short questionnaires I'd like you fill out. These will enable us to add significant value to you when we meet.

We're scheduled to meet on Wednesday, January 13 at 9:00 a.m. in our offices. We're located at 250 Lonsdale, on the ground floor. You'll find parking right next door; just bring in the ticket and we'll look after it for you. My assistant, Mary Jones, will confirm the meeting on Tuesday.

At our meeting, I would like to understand your situation in more depth. We will talk about those 'life transitions' we all go through and how those will affect your financial situation. In addition, I'd like to explore financial issues you feel are important to you today and in the future. We do not normally make financial recommendations until we have all of the information we need to let us make an informed recommendation. We trust you'll appreciate our Life-First advisory approach.

For more information on how we do what we do, visit our website at www.[address].com. By the way, please take a look at the links we've provided to some valuable life planning information for you!

Yours Sincerely

John Jones
Investment Advisor
ABC Financial

Enclosures: Introducing the John Jones Approach

Pre-Meeting Letter to a current client

John Jones
123 My Street
Toronto, ON
M8X 2Y2

<first name> <last name>
<address>
<city>, <province>
<postal code>

Dear <first name>:

As the needs of our long-time clients change, we feel it's important to provide advice that remains relevant and meets their needs. We would like to move our discussions with you towards how your financial plan affects your life plan.

We call this approach a Life-First Approach, which simply means that we make every effort to learn as much as we can about the way your financial situation can positively impact your life and the lives of your family.

We take a lot of pride in the way we help clients and feel it sets us apart from the many financial advisors available to you.

You will find everything we do with our clients relates financial planning to the much broader issues affecting their lives. You'll also see the seminars we provide for our clients, the newsletter we write and the way we conduct our financial planning process all focus on helping you 'turn success into significance'.

I've enclosed a brief overview of our approach as well as updates on our team and our philosophy. We hope you'll go through it as it will give you a good picture of the kind of understanding we will be seeking from you. In addition, I've enclosed two short questionnaires I would like you to look at and fill out if possible. They will form part of our discussion when we meet.

We're scheduled to meet on Wednesday January 13 at 9:00AM in our offices. Mary Jones will confirm the meeting on Tuesday.

At our meeting, I would like to talk about those 'life transitions' we all go through and how they will affect your financial situation. In addition, I would like to explore those financial issues you feel are important to you today and in the future that we may not be addressing.

By the way, we've recently upgraded our website at www.[address].com to reflect our Life-First Advisor focus. I'd appreciate your comments after you visit the site. By the way, take a look at some of the links we've provided to some valuable life planning information for you!

Regards,

Jack Jones
Investment Advisor
ABC Financial

Enclosures: Introducing the John Jones Approach

7 | Life-First Discovery

- **Life-First Discovery focuses on life issues before financial issues**
- **Clients view money as a means to an end, not an end in itself**
- **This approach helps differentiate yourself and your business**
- **By being client-centric, you build trust and reinforce discipline**

What if we could show you a way to *really* learn about your client, one that's a natural fit with your current role; a way that increases trust, confidence and the value you deliver and, as a result, gives you greater share-of-wallet?

What if you could use this unique process to set you apart from your peers?

We believe an effective client discovery process goes far beyond the normal financial questions on an account application form or a risk-tolerance questionnaire. It should not only seek to understand the client's money issues but also the personal, family and social issues that impact and influence their financial decisions.

Life-First Discovery is a departure from most discovery systems because of its focus on life issues before financial issues. We believe that if you understand a client's life issues you're better placed to understand their financial needs and goals.

We call it Life-First Discovery because it provides both the advisor and the client a complete and comprehensive life view and the impact that wealth planning can have.

In contrast, the traditional 'Portfolio First' approach yields all the information needed for investing but little life information. This makes it a challenge to develop a relevant, comprehensive wealth plan. It also tends to make advisors look alike, all asking the same questions and delivering the same results.

The Life-First Discovery process changes all this. It is specifically designed to help build trust and confidence in the mind of your client.

With this process, you learn about your clients' deepest goals, hopes, and challenges, even fears. You will ask questions the client may never have been asked before and understand them at a much deeper level than their other financial professionals.

This will help you build a better, more thorough wealth plan. It will also serve as the foundation for differentiating yourself from your peers. Above all, it will empower you to offer a better experience for your clients.

A framework for understanding

When you use a Life-First Discovery approach you are communicating that your practice centers on the client. In fact, you want to understand everything possible about the client that relates directly to the issues you're helping them with.

This tells your clients you care about them as people rather than as a 'sale'. That makes sense because if you claim to be a fiduciary and someone who always act in their clients' best interests you need to have a clear understanding of what those interests are.

There are several strong reasons to consider a Life-First Discovery process:

The older your clients, the more emotional they tend to be. As we age, we come to grips with mortality, confront hormonal issues and seek self-actualization. This means we tend to respond more to non-material issues such as family, health, leisure and emotional comfort. Life-First Discovery is an effective way to uncover these emotional issues.

Clients view their financial issues in real-life terms. Often a client's view on money reflects their advisor's view. Money is considered in a vacuum, separate from the life it serves. Helping clients view money as a means to an end rather than as an end in itself helps differentiate you from other financial advisors, and positions you as a trusted advisor.

Trust builds with understanding. When clients feel a personal, emotional connection with you, rather than just a financial connection, they tend to follow your guidance more closely and require less behavioral guidance.

The process differentiates you. While clients may respond to your marketing efforts, their comfort and confidence are derived mainly from their interactions with you. If you use the Life-First Discovery system effectively, your clients will walk out of a meeting thinking: 'I learned a lot about myself today. No one else has asked me those questions or helped me clarify issues I'd never even thought of'.

The process

We recommend a structured planning approach that helps clients identify and maintain their long-term goals without being derailed by emotional responses to short-term market activity. The best way to help them stay focused and on track is by using a structured, client-centric Life-First Process.

The most important step of this process is Life-First Discovery, because it drives the client's overall investment or wealth plan. Here's the basic outline of each step:

Meeting 1 – Clarity
This is your first meeting with someone who wants to be a client. You make use of two right-brain tools to help the client – and you – clarify the issues and the expectations for the relationship. At the end of this meeting, look at the financial documents the client has brought to ensure you have the information you need.

Meeting 2 – Insight and implementation
In this meeting, you outline your suggestions to your client and secure agreement to implement all or part of them.

Meeting 3+ – Ongoing partnership

You and your client agree on a meeting schedule for the next year. Be sure to schedule the first follow-up within the next month or two to discuss initial implementation.

Let's look at each of these in more detail.

The Clarity Meeting

You'll want the client to do some 'homework' by way of a self-discovery piece before this meeting, so try not to schedule it hard on the heels of the prospect meeting. There are four steps to the Clarity Meeting:

A Four-Step Process

1   Set the Stage

2   The Expectations Conversation

3   Conduct the Values Discussion

4   Summarize Agree Prioritize

Step 1 *– Set the Stage*

It's important to have a process. It's also important to have the client know you have a process. So now's the time to give your client a roadmap. This is a chance to showcase your approach and to establish the areas you'll be exploring. There should be no surprises. The client should never think, "Where is she going with this question?"

Setting the stage occurs at the outset of your planning meeting. Let the new client know how you work. You should cover the following:

- You are going to help the client create a personal wealth plan that will reflect the lifestyle goals and aspirations he has set for himself.

- You need to understand areas of the client's life that will be important when you create a plan and you'll spend some time getting to know the client first. To help you do that, you'll introduce the 'Life Picture' as a way to focus the discussion.

- The work you do with clients involves understanding the financial implications of the life issues they face. The next stage of your discovery process will help you understand the planning issues to address. You'll help the client visualize some of these issues when you introduce the 'Financial Life Map'.

- The 'Values Map' focuses on five key areas for your client to consider, plus any other areas they want to focus on. The discussion that flows from the Values Map uncovers lifestyle issues, goals and concerns first and then develops a wealth advisory strategy that reflects those. Ensure the client understands there is an important reason for each question.

At the end of this step you should ask your clients if they are comfortable with your approach to the creation of his wealth plan. If you don't establish these elements at the outset, your clients may subsequently think:

- "He's just like everyone else."

- "He's only concerned with money and he plans in a vacuum."

- "I have no idea why he's asking me that question."

- "Where is this going?"

- "How does this affect my life?"

- "I'm not going to share personal information – it isn't relevant."

You'll enhance trust if clients feel confident you have a system for discovery and they understand that system. Therefore, setting the stage is an important element in creating your value proposition.

Step 2 – The Expectations Conversation (15 minutes)

The Life Picture

The 'Life Picture' is a way to focus the discussion when seeking to understand areas of the client's life that will be important when you create a plan.

Pose this question to the client: "If we were meeting here five years from now and looking back, what great things would you have accomplished personally and professionally in these areas?"

It is five years from now...

"We have worked together for five years, what great things have you accomplished during your retirement?"

A good way to address the client's issues is to gain a '30,000-foot view' of their situation. There are seven basic areas of a client's life that directly relate to the financial plans you create. If you achieve a general understanding of those areas and use them to get clients to talk about their lives, you'll know where to go with the next part of the discussion.

Here's a tool that will focus the client on these key areas. Ask them a couple of questions related to each area:

Vision and Values
- What are the important values that drive how you view your money?
- What do you want to accomplish with the money you have?
- What things will be most important to you in the next phase of your life?
- What hopes do you have for you and your family?
- What will your life look like in the future?
- What would you like to accomplish with the financial resources you have?
- When you think of your retirement, what vision comes to mind?

Health
- What issues concern you about your health or the health of your family?
- What changes do you see occurring in your family health situation?
- What plans have you made in the event of a health challenge?

Work
- What will you miss most about the work you do?
- How did your career evolve to this point?
- What would you like to do if you didn't have the job you do now?
- What plans do you have for retirement that may include work – paid or not?

Family
- Tell me about your family...
- What family issues should we consider when making a plan?
- Will caregiving be an issue for you at some point?
- Who else in your family will be affected by the plans we put in place?

Leisure

- How do you like to spend your time when you're not working?
- If you had more free time how would you use it?
- Have you thought about how much travel you'd like to do?
- What are your plans for a vacation home?
- How do you see spending your time when you're not traveling?

Home

- Do you expect to stay in your current home for a long time?
- What would have to happen for you to reconsider where you live?
- Have you thought about where you'll live in your retirement?
- What would you change about where you live now?
- What concerns you about how your home will meet your needs as you get older?

Financial Comfort

- What worries you about your future financial situation?
- What do you want your money to do for you?
- How would you like to see your spiritual beliefs reflected in the plan?
- How would you like to use your money in ways you're not doing today?
- What kinds of financial issues might keep you up at night?
- What would make you comfortable in your day-to-day financial situation?
- What are the biggest mistakes you feel you make?

The expectations discussion doesn't have to be lengthy. You want to move to financial discovery and the Values Map as soon as you can, but you also want to respect the client's lifestyle issues first. If there is information you don't get out of the lifestyle discussion, you can always circle back later.

The key at this stage is that you're gaining a general understanding of the client. Keep the discussion focused on life, not money issues.

You now want the client to prioritize the life areas that concern them the most and build them into the plan. Ask clients to pick the top two or three areas from this part of the discussion that they think should be a priority as you shift to values discovery.

"It's been insightful getting a good overview of your life and the things we should consider as we build a plan. Now I'd like to shift gears and focus on the areas where I feel we can help you tie your financial resources to your life areas."

Step 3 — *The Values Map (40 minutes)*

The Values Map is financial discovery with a difference. It helps identify the real, emotional underpinnings below clients' financial planning issues. Indeed, the pure financial areas often pale in comparison with the hard life issues clients face.

Use the Values Map to uncover potential planning areas before tying those life issues to the financial resources available to look after them. Of course, each client will place weight on different issues, and there will always be discussion points that are not relevant to a particular client.

As the retiring client looks to the future, what emotional issues will affect how they look at their money? What do they want their financial resources to do for them and their families now they are moving into this next phase of their lives?

You should move through the discussion points below in order, addressing the major topic area first. Not all will be applicable, but it helps the client to see the overall picture even so.

Here's a possible script:
"Let's go through the major areas that we'll have to consider as we develop a plan together. My questions will focus on two things: Where are you now in this area? And what do you see happening in the future that we'll need to plan for?

The key here is to get the client to think in terms of the gap between where they are today and where they need to be. Since the discussion points are meant to be general conversation areas you can take the discussion anywhere the client needs it to go to visualize the future.

Let's talk about ...

Helping and protecting family. There are few more emotional issues than family. It's normally best to start here and uncover what issues the client feels are most important.

Enjoying and protecting lifestyle. Focus here on issues that have a financial consequence. These would range from income generation or replacement to the client's 'bucket list.' Consider health issues.

Planning for the expected and unexpected. Generally, life transition issues such as retirement, disability and career change are areas that may cause disruption or change to the financial plans currently in place.

Creating financial comfort. This considers how the client feels about concepts such as 'money', 'risk' and the role of the advisor. Keep this towards the end of the discovery process as it is more about tactics than strategy. The focus here is on specific issues such as managing the portfolio or tax planning.

Building a legacy. This is the last area for discussion and focuses on such topics as the will, estate plan and charitable giving. This doesn't have to be a negative discussion, and it is necessary. It works better as a bookend to the plan you put together in the other areas.

Step 4 – Summarizing the Clarity Meeting

The best way to summarize the discussion is to work with the client to prioritize issues in four categories:

Needs: These are the areas that should be dealt with immediately.

Wants: These tend to emerge out of your discussion.

Wishes: These are 'stretch' goals that can be achieved with the right strategies.

Goals: A summation of life goals. Normally, the advisor would start here and then divide them up into the other three categories.

Summarizing the Discussion

Needs	Wants	Wishes	Goals

The advantage of these tools and your discovery process is that you have a foundation for a continuing discussion with your client by using the same approach each time.

Some advisors customize the Values Map for regular meetings by color-coding the boxes based on

- Issues we need to discuss today.

- Issues that are ongoing and which need to be updated.

- Issues not applicable or already handled.

Of course, you can change titles in the financial discovery visual to fit the client's particular circumstance. Under this approach, there are four planning issues that affect your client:

Accumulating Wealth. This refers to the client's need to build assets for life goals such as retirement, education and house purchase. Wealth accumulation begins when an individual first has excess discretionary income.

Advisor challenges in this area include:

- Considering other motivations as the client moves out of this stage.
- Ensuring the client understands the relationship between accumulating assets and using them for life enjoyment.

Your questions:

- What does the client want for the future?

- How much can they put aside?

- How much will they need to achieve their goals?

- What will make them lose sleep at night?

Protecting Wealth. This refers to the client's need to preserve what they have and to ensure their assets are protected from the unforeseen. Insurance and tax planning are key elements. The need to protect wealth starts from the time assets start to accumulate but becomes even more important when accumulation starts to become less of a priority.

Advisor challenges in this area include:

- Making sure the financial planning discussion includes reference to wealth protection.
- Ensuring the client understands that protecting wealth also means protecting lifestyle.

Your questions:

- What does the client need to protect?
- How can they manage risk to achieve what they see as financial comfort?
- What life changes do they foresee that you can protect against?

Converting Wealth to an Income Stream. There comes a point when a client's regular income will flow from the financial resources they've created and protected. Efficiently and effectively creating an income stream draws in insurance and tax planning elements that the client may not always understand or appreciate.

Advisor challenges in this area include:

- Protecting as much income as possible from tax.
- Blending income into existing pension plans or entitlement programs.
- Educating the client on alternatives available to convert wealth to income.

Your questions:

- How much is enough?
- Where will it come from?
- What unexpected things need to be planned for?

Transferring Wealth. Legacy issues aren't always estate planning issues. In fact, many clients seek to use their financial resources to create living legacies through benevolence or helping family.

Advisor challenges in this area include:

- Creating the discussion on the opportunities to create a legacy.
- Educating the client on the available options.

Your questions:

- What is their plan?
- Are they seeking to help children or parents?
- What about charitable giving?
- Do they want to create a living legacy?
- How can they protect their estate?

Once you have all the information you need from the discovery process, you can proceed to analysis and devising solutions.

Remember, the wealth discovery process works best if you don't try to deliver strategy in the same meeting. You want to demonstrate that you will take the information and thoroughly consider the options. This is not something typically achieved via a quick glance at a client's investment portfolio.

So, set a date and time for the next meeting, agree on any additional information that may be needed, discuss other resources the client can access, and let the client know you'll provide them with further information as necessary.

Recording information

A challenge in meetings is the need to balance note taking with the eye-to-eye contact required to create an emotional connection.

Your primary goal is to gain understanding and maintain rapport. In fact, the need to create a bond is more important in these initial stages of client discovery than remembering all the information.

So, don't worry about capturing every piece of information. Whatever you miss you can always come back to later. You can also fill in the blanks when you're analyzing the client's balance sheet and other financial information.

Your notes should consist of as much 'shorthand' as you need to make sure you pay attention to the client.

Organize the information using a simple template. You can also use a summary to combine both the expectations and values discussions.

Some advisors use a small tape recorder during the meeting. The positives are that you can maintain eye contact and not miss anything. The negatives are that the client may feel uncomfortable or concerned about privacy of potentially very personal information. Some compliance officers will not allow taping at all. Others demand custodial safeguards for client information to avoid private information being easily accessible.

You could use a third party as a note taker, freeing you up to focus on the client. This also helps younger advisors as they learn the process. On the flipside, you may be the better judge of what information is worth noting.

An effective way to gather information is to stop at regular intervals and summarize your understanding on a notepad or whiteboard with your client. You could say, "Let's take a few minutes to ensure I've heard you and understand the key issues."

The advantage is twofold. First, you're involving the client in your note taking and jointly creating the summary. That helps reinforce the issues and concerns in the mind of the client. Second, your client feels more engaged in the process and it reinforces your collaborative and coaching approach.

The Insight Meeting

The goal now is to move the process forward, either by agreeing on next steps or implementing part or all of the plan. The driver will be the meeting summary, which is the working document for the advisor and client to implement a plan.

Here are some possible financial solutions in the US that we have tied to the Values Map. These can be customized for your market.

Discovery Insight and Solutions (example)

Some solutions that flow from the values discussion

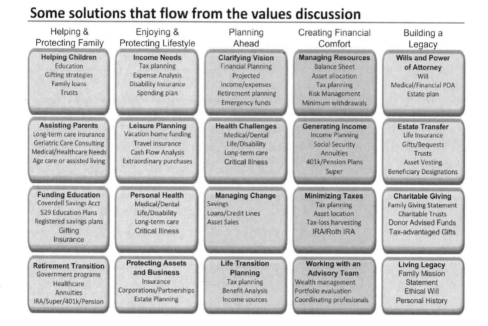

Helping & Protecting Family	Enjoying & Protecting Lifestyle	Planning Ahead	Creating Financial Comfort	Building a Legacy
Helping Children Education Gifting strategies Family loans Trusts	**Income Needs** Tax planning Expense Analysis Disability Insurance Spending plan	**Clarifying Vision** Financial Planning Projected income/expenses Retirement planning Emergency funds	**Managing Resources** Balance Sheet Asset allocation Tax planning Risk Management Minimum withdrawals	**Wills and Power of Attorney** Will Medical/Financial POA Estate plan
Assisting Parents Long-term care insurance Geriatric Care Consulting Medical/Healthcare Needs Age care or assisted living	**Leisure Planning** Vacation home funding Travel insurance Cash Flow Analysis Extraordinary purchases	**Health Challenges** Medical/Dental Life/Disability Long-term care Critical Illness	**Generating Income** Income Planning Social Security Annuities 401k/Pension Plans Super	**Estate Transfer** Life Insurance Gifts/Bequests Trusts Asset Vesting Beneficiary Designations
Funding Education Coverdell Savings Acct 529 Education Plans Registered savings plans Gifting Insurance	**Personal Health** Medical/Dental Life/Disability Long-term care Critical Illness	**Managing Change** Savings Loans/Credit Lines Asset Sales	**Minimizing Taxes** Tax planning Asset location Tax-loss harvesting IRA/Roth IRA	**Charitable Giving** Family Giving Statement Charitable Trusts Donor Advised Funds Tax-advantaged Gifts
Retirement Transition Government programs Healthcare Annuities IRA/Super/401k/Pension	**Protecting Assets and Business** Insurance Corporations/Partnerships Estate Planning	**Life Transition Planning** Tax planning Benefit Analysis Income sources	**Working with an Advisory Team** Wealth management Portfolio evaluation Coordinating profesionals	**Living Legacy** Family Mission Statement Ethical Will Personal History

Present recommendations in a positive, strategic, action-oriented way. There are two kinds of tools available to help:

Visioning software can be used in the discovery process itself to help a client see the big picture, clarify goals or introduce issues.

Planning software is numbers driven and provides the advisor with a format in which to present the final plan.

Ongoing meetings

Finally, you'll discuss with the client how regularly – and how – they wish to interact over the next year. Schedule the first follow-up meeting within the next month or two as you start to look at the implementation of strategy.

Remember, you'll want to stay 'top of mind' and build a true partnership.

The Life-First Advisor ...

- Treats discovery as a conversation not an inquisition
- Makes good use of coaching questions
- Has separate Prospect, Clarity and Insight Meetings
- Finds a way to take notes that still allows 'connection' with the client

8 | Presenting Your Ideas

- **In presenting ideas, target the right brain first**
- **The key is getting the client to internalize the information**
- **Concentrate information at the tip of the iceberg**
- **Go deeper if the client requires more detail**
- **Be aware of the concerns underlying the question**

Whether you're presenting to a client in your office, to a pension fund policy committee or to 100 clients at a seminar, there's an effective way to make your points while respecting the way your audience processes information.

In cognitive psychology, 'scaffolding' refers to how effective educators layer a message in a way that helps the audience internalize it. It's the same way young children learn language and it's consistent with our concept of client self-discovery.

Earlier, we noted that the brain can work against the learning or focusing process if you don't make it as easy as possible for it to do so.

Two roadblocks prevent advisors presenting or explaining something effectively. First, they feel that as long as they're speaking the audience is listening and connecting the dots. This 'if I build it, they will come' approach to communication is not an effective way to maintain the audience's attention.

Second, advisors often believe the smarter or more successful the client the less the need to respect brain science. "My clients are engineers", said one. "They immediately process information and come to quick conclusions because that's how they think". Other advisors might feel the more financially literate a client is the more 'left brain' the discussion should be.

The truth is this isn't about financial literacy, affluence or business success. It's about capturing audience attention, turning on the emotional light switches in the right brain and getting people to internalize the information. In short, use your presentation to 'get them thinking' and to become internally focused.

Think of the audience as a sponge. You could tip a bucket of water on the sponge and it would absorb some of it. Alternatively, you could slowly pour the water to the point where it has absorbed all of it. Use the scaffolding concept to slowly add information. This way the responding brain is more likely to start internalizing it.

The Iceberg Metaphor

The Iceberg

What **most** clients want to know

What **many** advisors do

What **some** clients want to know

What **few** clients want to know

The Life-First Advisor is a communicator who speaks in plain language and seeks to simplify things as much as possible. Brain science tells us people are more likely to pay attention to a message if they don't have to work hard to process it.

However, that's not to say you shouldn't include some left-brain, detail-focused information.

Another advisor we worked with was revamping his client brochure and website with the aim of giving clients and prospects an outline of the value he brings.

"I want them to know that I have a lot of experience and that I have a thorough and systematic approach to investment management", he told us. "One of the things I'm most proud of is my eight-step investment process and I want to make sure this is reflected in my brochure."

Now, ask yourself how many clients and prospects are really interested in an eight-step investment management process? Do they all want to know the details about how the advisor chooses investments? How much does an advisor have to explain to clients to build trust and gain their confidence?

The answer to the last question is easy – the advisor has to explain to clients as much as they want to know. That simply means the explanation has to be geared to each client, rather than assuming everyone wants every detail.

The 'deep dive' approach of many advisors reminds us of icebergs, which are typically about 90 percent below the water. Most clients only want to know what's above the water line. Their message is: 'Tell me what I *need* to know and why I should care'. Yet many advisors deluge clients with the stuff below, almost as if they feel the more detail they provide the smarter and more professional they look.

Of course, some clients will want more and you should be ready to explore the depths if they ask. Just don't assume everyone wants the same degree of detail.

Our suggestion is to ask for permission. For example, when explaining your preferred investment approach, say: *"I have this investment piece I'd like to talk about – would you like the short version, the medium version or the long version?"*

We can tell you from experience that the vast majority of clients opt for the short version. If they have any questions, they'll let you know. This way you save a lot of time and the client is spared a great deal of tedium.

Likewise, if you're writing a brochure or newsletter, it's best to focus on general information than to assume all your readers are CFA-qualified.

In the case of the advisor above, our suggestion was to focus on his overall investment philosophy. That description should be relayed in layperson's terms and focus on how the advisor's process benefits the client.

Here's an example: *"My philosophy is to understand your specific needs and then tailor an investment management plan to you. I take a systematic and disciplined approach to managing your nest egg and work with you to make changes when necessary to reflect your personal situation."*

That above-the-waterline explanation will satisfy most people because they'll feel confident the advisor has a process and is building something specifically for them.

Other clients will want to go to the second layer of the iceberg for more detail on how the advisor's money management process works. Some are just interested in investment. Others want to feel confident the advisor knows what they're doing.

So a second-level explanation might be: *"My view is asset allocation is the key. I tilt your portfolio towards the drivers of higher expected returns and diversify broadly. I rebalance when your personal situation changes or when market moves shift you out of your chosen risk profile."*

The eight-step process would be found on the third level. If the client wants to go there you should be willing to explain it to them. However it makes little sense to start with a deep dive before you're certain the client is that interested.

Generally, when you use industry buzzwords or talk in 'advisor speak', you're going below the water line and do so at your peril. You risk losing the client's attention and their ability to internalize the information you're providing. So focus on why the client should care. In terms of the benefits of your advice, don't confuse what you do (above the water line) with how you do it (below).

The iceberg and tough questions

The first thing you need to identify is the *real* question behind the one the client is asking. That will determine how deep you have to go. Here's an example:

The client asks: "Can you explain what a wealth advisor does and why I should do business with you rather than someone else?"

The underlying question is: "I haven't had a great experience in the past and I didn't see any value from my previous advisors. All firms seem to do the same thing. How are you different?".

Your 'tip of the iceberg' response: "Other advisors manage money. We focus first on understanding the things in life that are important to you. Only then do we create the strategies that fit your needs. And we only work with a select group of clients who would benefit from that approach."

Your second-level response: "We take an evidence-based approach to designing solutions and strategies. This is a strategic rather than tactical approach. It's goal-driven and proactive rather than reactive. In drawing up a plan we focus on those factors that can be controlled, and on what works rather than what 'sells'."

Your third-level response: We assess your life situation, goals, risk appetite and circumstances and work back from there to design an asset allocation. That means a diversified global portfolio built around equities, fixed income, property and cash. We tailor it from there depending on your needs, while focusing on minimizing costs and controlling for tax effects. We rebalance half-yearly. The investment component complements the overall risk and lifestyle assessment, which we review regularly."

In an appendix at the end of this book we provide a table that looks at some other questions you might face and how to address them.

The 2-3-1 formula

When presenting three points to an audience – a number that tends to work well – there's a way to position those points to take advantage of how the brain works.

Imagine you're outlining three benefits of what you do, each of varying benefit. Most communicators would lead with the best benefit first, followed by the second most attractive and then the least important benefit. Here's a more effective way:

Start with the benefit that's the *second* most attractive. This will likely have some interest for the client and they'll start to think about this point.

Follow with your *least* important benefit. Your listener is most likely still focusing on the first benefit. If they've 'checked out' on your first point they may not pay as much attention to your second point anyway.

Conclude with your *best* possible benefit. This is the one the client will find most important and the one you want to emphasize. Ensure the listener doesn't miss it by introducing it with words like 'and best of all...'

Remember, you're trying to turn on the emotional light switches in the right brain to get your message across and your clients thinking.

The Life-First Advisor ...

- Lays out information so the right brain or emotional center processes it first
- Gives only as much information as the listener wants or can cope with
- Starts 'above the water line' then works down

9 | Taking Your Message to the Market

- It's not enough to just say you are now a Life-First Advisor
- The next step is marketing your message across a broad front
- Clients should be able to articulate your value
- Define your proposition in terms of what you do for people

Noted Chinese philosopher Sun Tsu was quoted in *The Art of War*: "If you can't win on the battlefield you are on, find a battlefield where you can win and fight the battle there!"

For today's financial professional, the challenge is to find a battlefield that not only defines you but which sets you apart from your competition. That's why branding is so important in setting yourself out from the crowd.

The concept of holistic planning isn't new. Some advisors have sought to relate life planning and financial planning throughout their careers. Many others, though, while knowing this approach is important, don't know how to do it.

As a result, holistic planning has not entered the mainstream or been used much as a differentiator. But that's about to change as the advice industry remakes itself in response to the demands of an aging clientele.

As Bob Veres of *Dow Jones Investment Advisor* noted: "I think we should be careful about ignoring the growing Life Planning movement.

Financial advisors, in our view, are the very best qualified people on the planet to help their clients enjoy better and more fulfilling lives. Whether or not we jump on board, Life Planning is going to become increasingly important to the financial planning profession."

It's a perspective shared by industry consultant Dan Richards of ClientInsights, who has worked with thousands of advisors and their firms over the past 20 years: "I am always amazed how many advisors overestimate their clients' perception of the value that they bring to the table," he said.

The result is advisors are not paying enough attention to how to differentiate themselves from their competitors.

It's one thing for the advisor to develop a unique, personalized approach to financial planning and client service. It's quite another for them to develop a communications strategy that ensures the audience 'gets it'.

On this score, it's worth pointing out the fundamental difference between selling and marketing. Selling is about getting the client to understand the benefit of your advice to them. Marketing refers to all of the activities both before and after the selling interaction that create an image in the mind of the client about the advisor.

Richards sums up the distinction this way: "Selling involves convincing someone that you have what they want; marketing is making sure that you have what somebody wants."

So the key question to ask is what your clients and prospects want today. The table below lists a few things the average client might want. Use it to rank your clients' need for these services and your ability to provide them.

Service a client or prospect might need	How important is this to clients and prospects (High, Medium, Low)	Do you provide this in some way now? (Yes or No)	Do your clients look to you for this service?	How do you communicate to the market-place that you provide this service?
Information on lifestyle planning				
Help or information on goal setting				
Understanding of key life transition issues				
Understanding the financial implications of life planning decisions				
Access to information on non-financial, life-oriented education				
Introductions to non-financial professionals such as personal trainers, psychologists				
Information on career transition or other work-related topics				
Information on non-financial aspects associated with retirement				

You might respond to this list by saying you're not in the business of life plans but about helping clients understand the financial implications of their life decisions.

If that's the case, ask yourself what it is about the service you provide now that sets you apart from your competition?

Services you provide	Can your clients get this somewhere else?	How do they see you as different to other advisors?
Facilitate transactions		
Provide financially oriented products		
Develop financial plans		
Provide financial or investment information		
Provide tax advice		
Specialize in a specific financial planning area		

From a marketing perspective it's not enough to provide the service. The client or prospect needs to view the service as different or better than that available elsewhere. If you aren't able to articulate how you set yourself apart it will be very difficult to market what makes you distinctive.

Given the commoditization of financial services, including most of the items on the list above, how do you differentiate yourself?

This is why the Life-First Approach is an important branding opportunity, not only in taking more of a lifestyle and transition-based planning approach but in being *seen* to be taking that approach.

At a recent workshop, one advisor who had taken a certification program on elder studies lamented that this effort had been wasted. "There hasn't been any direct benefit to me at all", he said. "I still do the same things for my clients and I don't see any changes in the way that I run my practice."

Asked what kinds of things he'd done to market his specialization, he was unable to say. He hadn't changed his firm's brochure or his business card, nor had he run seminars on elder planning issues. He was taking the 'if I build it, they will come' approach, thinking prospects and clients would somehow just get it.

Your brand should be your 'secret sauce', providing people with a way to classify your value proposition. Yet many financial advisors have a brand that is either tied up with the company they license through or work for or is suggested by what they call themselves:

"I am a wealth manager".
"I am a financial planner".
"I am an insurance specialist".
"I am an investment advisor".

The problem with these descriptors is they don't really say what you do in a way that separates you from everyone else. Let's say you're the best, most knowledgeable insurance specialist in the country. Can you advertise that in a way that's not only compliant but in a way that makes your marketplace *believe* it?

Take an office of 30 advisors with potentially 6,000 clients. If you surveyed all those clients, how many definitions of what a financial planner does would you get? Maybe 6,000 and 30 more from the advisors?

There's your challenge. How do you make yourself look different if you're not really doing something else? The answer is simple: do something different and then make sure your marketplace knows it.

Where brand marketing goes wrong

There are three basic reasons why advisors don't succeed when taking their brand to the market:

They don't personally buy into the brand. These advisors have never articulated what the brand means and how to apply it to their marketplace. Often, they look at their brand as simply another way to label their practice without realizing it is the public face of the methodology. The Life-First Approach means reinforcing the brand at every opportunity.

They try to be 'all things to all people'. This dilutes the brand. These advisors change their brand depending on whom they're talking to. They have a hard time defining their approach or their marketplace and, of course, their marketplace has a hard time recognizing their brand.

They take the 'if I build it, they will come' approach. Just because you say you have a brand doesn't necessarily mean your marketplace will pick up on it. Your brand has to be disseminated according to an overall strategy that includes your communications package, what your clients see during your interactions with them, and how you send your message to your marketplace.

Three keys to brand awareness

Three crucial elements must be in place for the advisor's 'brand' to register with the client:

The client must understand what needs the advisor meets. These needs can be short-term ("I need more insurance on my business") or long-term ("I need a savings program for my child's college education"). Most advisors set themselves out as 'problem solvers'. This is certainly important in facilitating transactions but it doesn't imbed the advisor's brand in the mind of the client.

The client must have an emotional attachment to the advisor's practice. Remember, buying decisions are made in the right brain or emotional center, not in the rational left brain. The right brain is also the home of long-term memory, which means the client must feel an emotional attachment to the advisor if there's to be a long-term relationship. Emotional attachment means the client feels such things as comfort, security, happiness, joy, knowledge, understanding and caring. If not, then you're a vendor not a partner.

The client must be able to articulate exactly what the advisor does for them. Many advisors assume their clients could list two or three things that set the advisor apart and give them a special place in the mind of the client. In fact, most clients only have a general sense that they like their advisor and would have difficulty telling a friend exactly why.

Communicating your brand

Brand reinforcement simply means letting your clients know over and over again what it is you're doing for them and why you are different. Some advisors will say, "But my clients will remember what I do for them. Why do I have to keep telling them what is so obvious?"

The answer is that you want to reinforce the emotional attachment the client has with you in any way possible. By continuing to provide them with consistent communication that outlines your special approach to them, you're firmly entrenching your brand in their consciousness.

Remember, you want them to be able to list three reasons why they deal with you, hopefully to anyone who will listen!

Your target market

Like any business owner, you need to identify the specific groups that will find your message appealing.

If your role is to help people relate life planning to financial planning, your focus will be those individuals who are already contemplating their own life plans.

These people are looking for answers to their questions in many different places and may not view a financial planner as a source of information on the non-financial aspects of life planning.

There are several obvious groups who will be actively seeking help and support in their journeys of personal discovery:

- Anyone contemplating a significant life transition.
- Anyone coming to grips with a new phase of their life.
- Anyone trying to help someone going through such transitions.

As generational shifts occur earlier, later or not at all when compared to older generations and previous eras, individuals become much more introspective.

Many financial advisors are afraid to go outside their comfort zone and suggest they can provide life-related information, believing that's getting too personal. One such advisor summed it up by saying: "If I start sending out information on health or career transition or life planning to my clients, they're going to think I'm some kind of wing nut!"

On the one hand, you have a potential client who's trying to make sense out of life events such as turning 50, having their retirement plans go awry, or seeing their work or relationships change. On the other, you have a financial advisor who says "I'm only going to provide financial advice and service to the people who come to my office. Let them work their life problems out before they get here."

The fact is everyone is a target market for the Life-First Advisor because everyone goes through life changes. Most will have no idea whether or not they are on track to achieve their life goals and will be seeking insights.

An obvious opportunity using the Life-First approach is to help people understand the 'new retirement' they face because of the ageing population. This will affect anyone now aged between the ages of 35 and 60 – from those not as concerned about accumulating money as they are about making sense of 'middle' age through to the wave of baby boomers now hitting retirement.

Your marketing should focus on how you can help clients find their own answers, with the benefit of the information and expertise you can connect them with. This concept of the advisor as a 'human web browser' cuts across all potential target markets.

Introducing Life-First to existing clients

Your best source of future referrals is your present clientele, so it's just as important to market to them as it is to target prospective clients. While not all of your clients will change the way they perceive you, most will view you in a new or different light if you introduce the Life-First approach properly.

The challenge is how to let existing clients know you're taking a different approach.

Rather than providing a formal introduction to the program, some advisors opt to introduce select elements such as the Life-First Discovery process and hope the client notices the difference. This is an opportunity lost. As discussed, your clients must understand the Life-First Approach and be able to articulate what you do to their friends, family and business associates.

Here are some ways you can make the transition as natural and effective as possible:

Explain you are expanding your offering because of changing needs. You don't want to suggest there was a gap in your services, rather that you are formalizing something you've already been doing – with the aim of ensuring all your clients' needs are met, not just those related to investment.

Send a letter to your clients to let them know what you're doing and why, perhaps using the sample letter we included earlier in this book. Make sure all your clients receive your new brochure, along with the introduction letter.

Introduce the Life-First Approach in client update meetings. Immediately schedule client update meetings with your key clients to provide an opportunity to introduce your positioning.

Use a pre-meeting package or even video to present the concept before your next progress meeting. This package could contain your brochure, as well as an outline of the wealth advisory process you'll take in the upcoming meeting. A sample pre-meeting package and checklist is included in a later chapter.

Make use of the values map we introduced in client discovery and conduct a client re-discovery program. Here's a way you could introduce this to your client:

"George and Mary, we have worked together for the past seven years and have discussed many life issues that required an investment or wealth plan. As you move through the different stages of life, there will be new things that have to be considered – as well as things now forgotten or requiring clarification. I would like to use this outline of wealth planning to make sure we look at all areas. In fact, I am doing this with each of my clients as a way of ensuring we cover all the bases."

Implement an education program as quickly as possible. Hold a workshop or education session on a non-financial topic, inviting your key clients to attend. This is a chance to do a joint seminar with a potential professional referral source. Examples of workshops that would help you introduce your approach are:

- Retirement lifestyle planning
- Charitable giving opportunities
- Understanding long-term or critical care for your loved ones
- Fit after 50
- Turning Success into Significance – creating a legacy

You want attendees to know this session is part of an ongoing seminar program. The investment or financial product component of this workshop should be minor. It's important for you to speak at the workshop, to explain the Life-First Approach and why you have decided to expand your service offering.

We cover client education more fully in another chapter.

Create a client contact program that includes non-financial issues. You want your client to feel you are an ever-present and relevant part of their planning. Therefore, create client 'touches' that will continue to reinforce your Wealth Planning brand. Examples of things you can send to your clients are:

- Magazine articles on topics of interest – again, non-financial if possible but certainly focused on the key areas of wealth planning.

- Letters, one-pagers or emails on a topic relevant to your client.

Change the language you use to describe your service offering. Your transition to being a Life-First Advisor not only affects your financial planning methodology and the way you market yourself but also the way you communicate to your clients. Remember that if you use left-brain investment terms to describe what you do, you aren't reinforcing your brand.

Developing a Life-First marketing strategy

The Life-First Approach is a differentiation and branding strategy, along with a financial planning methodology. Therefore, the marketing approach has to set the advisor apart from others.

There are many ways to market yourself. Here are a few suggested approaches and the goal of each:

Value Proposition	Define your practice 'above the line' in terms of how you meet clients' immediate needs	Show how you work with clients to meet their needs; explain your expertise and level of support
Discovery Process	In a marketing sense, the discovery process is a way of showing how you take a different approach	Uncovering the clients' needs, concerns, opportunities and goals
Education Program	Inform attendees on how 'life objectives' link to 'financial strategies'.	Provides context on making better decisions and differentiates you
Social Media	Survey clients on social media and use these channels to enhance your relationships	Improves the depth and breadth of your communication, encouraging 'shares'
Website	Creates the 'feel' of your practice, using color, video, graphics etc	Confirms the emotion-based message you wish to send to your marketplace

Centers of Influence	Expand COIs beyond CPAs and lawyers. A COI is anyone who has the same client as you do	Creating loose or informal connections ensures everyone understands your service
Client Rediscovery	Use the financial life map to uncover things you didn't know about the client's life	Shows your life-based approach and creates cross-positioning opportunities
Client Advisory Boards	Create focus groups out of your top clients to provide input on how you can be more effective	Makes your clients feel they are a part of your practice and gives them the opportunity to help
Referral Campaign	Clients grasp what you do 'above the line' and how to describe it. Use a systemized approach and seek introductions	Creates name awareness and lets clients know they can help by introducing you to potential clients or COIs in their network
Media Campaign	Avoid paid advertising and aim for media 'earned' by sharing your expertise in specific areas	Creates brand awareness

The Life-First brand permeates the advisor's communications, seminars and workshops, newsletters, website and social media. As a result, clients and prospects are very clear on your approach.

So the key elements of an effective marketing strategy are:

- Your value proposition
- Your market identification or branding
- Your communications strategy with current clients
- Your prospecting strategy for new clients

In this book we have looked at each of these elements.

How far are you willing to go?

Here's a quick exercise to help you assess how far you're willing to 'push the envelope' when it comes to the life planning approach:

	No	*Maybe*	*Yes*
I am willing to use holistic planning (or objective, life-based planning) as a description of what I do for clients			
I will develop a pre-meeting package that helps my new client understand the life-based focus I take			
All my marketing material will position financial planning as a natural extension of the client's life planning			
I will develop a questionnaire to discover more about my client's family, goals and vision for retirement, as well as their views on money and its relationship to their lives.			
I will help my clients understand the life transitions they might face and the financial implications			
I will seek out professionals focused on their clients' non-financial issues and develop referral relationships with them			
My clients will be able to get information from my office on many different aspects of life planning			
I will conduct life planning-oriented seminars, workshops and events and use outside resources to provide expert information			
I will expand my database to include as much personal information on my clients as I can encourage them to share			
I will commit to working with fewer clients but will build more personal relationships with my key clients.			

The Life-First Advisor ...

- Understands the target market for the Life-First Approach
- Positions their practice to deliver a service that's different to that of most advisors
- Clearly communicates their difference to current clients as well as prospects
- Ensures all marketing and communications is 'right-brain' focused

10 | Your Client Contact Strategy

- An effective communication strategy is pivotal to your branding
- This is as much a marketing as a relationship management tool
- The key is delivering content of relevance
- Use everyday language that builds an emotional connection

At a financial advisor conference, a business journalist interviewing us about our presentation "How to Relate Clients' Money More Closely with their Lives" appeared confused about the need for such a message.

"I thought advisors related financial planning to the client's life plan as a matter of course", she said. "Why do you need to talk to advisors about how to do something that's part of their jobs anyway?"

It's true that many advisors believe they really *do* relate financial planning to their clients' dreams and goals. They ask life planning-oriented questions as part of their discovery process. Yet, the real magic of Life-First planning in building and nurturing the advisor-client relationship is often lost.

A US researcher found in a study of investors in 2014 that the two things most of them wanted from advisors were information and education. Many felt overloaded by external information, she found, and were looking for an honest broker to filter it.

But if you're going to play a more holistic role in your clients' lives beyond the purely financial, clients must see you as more than a 'money' professional.

That means the way you communicate to clients is probably more important in developing your role than the work you do in developing a financial plan.

Participants in a 2000 study of financial planners at a conference in the US found while many claimed to be using life planning, they were not perceived that way by their clients. Not even the larger firms with deep resources and enormous market reach had successfully communicated this approach.

The think tank behind the study said if life planning was to be seen to be valuable by people, the industry would need to address the message and the medium.

"It also will have to address individuals' and generational groups' deeply rooted feelings about money", the think tank said, "even as it seeks to distance money from life goals."

In retrospect, that seminal conference represented the first effort to quantify the life-based approach to financial advice.

The 3 goals of communication

Your communications strategy should serve three main goals:

It should provide clients with thought-provoking information on life issues. Your information may stimulate the client's thinking about the future and provide a fertile ground to consider other perspectives. A way to do this is by providing a steady flow of thought-provoking material.

It should show that the life plan is a foundation for wealth management. If you start providing life-oriented information rather than just financial information, you're showing your clients you care about their wider lives beyond material concerns.

It should act as a point of differentiation. How will you separate yourself from your competition in the future? What is it that sets you apart in the minds of your clients and what do they say to their friends and family about what it is you do for them?

The Life-first approach is turning marketing and communication on its head. Ten years ago, the client mindset was 'I'll stay unless you give me a reason to go'. Today, more and more clients say that, regardless of your history together, they'll *go* unless you give them a reason to *stay*."

The number one imperative for advisors will be delivering outstanding value, not as defined by them but as defined by their clients. Furthermore, the things which have represented value and have differentiated advisors until now will be no more than "me too."

So if you can use the information you provide for clients to add value in their lives you'll have gone a long way towards bullet proofing the relationship.

The question is what constitutes added value? The precise answer will depend on the client, but it's safe to assume they'll look to you as a source of information and education.

Assessing your strategy

The information you provide should focus on meeting each client's individual needs. By definition, life planning is a personal thing. It requires a relationship where clients feel safe enough to receive more focused information relevant to their particular situation.

This personal connection can scare off some advisors who are reluctant to move beyond the sharing of financial information towards a new, broader role. This is what leads advisors to crowd their newsletters, website, seminars and workshops with information about mutual funds and investments.

We recommend you review the information you provide and ask yourself whether it really is valuable to the client. You can use a number of criteria in undertaking this review:

- How relevant is the information to your clients' lives?
- What kind of feedback do you receive from your communications?
- Does the information set you apart from your competition?
- How do you think your clients think about this material?

Communication Tools

Pre-Discovery Meeting Package		As needed	
Focused client education workshops		Bi-weekly or monthly	
Public seminars		Quarterly	
Update letters (can be delivered electronically)		As needed	
Regular statements		Quarterly	
Client appreciation events		Semi-annually	
Regular phone calls (including 'no reason' calls)		At least monthly for 'A's and 'B's	
Regular progress meetings		Quarterly for 'A's and 'B's, semi-annually for rest	
Articles or email blasts		Once a month	
Brochures		These replace or are in addition to business cards	
Newsletters		Quarterly	
Website		Ongoing	
Twitter		Ongoing	
YouTube		Add content to your channel regularly	
Facebook		Keep it fresh and updated as needed	
LinkedIn		Daily	

Let's look at some of the key tools for communication.

Your website

As with every other communication method, your website should express your brand clearly and consistently.

- Your point of differentiation should be prominent.
- The design and navigation should be simple and intuitive.
- To be distinctive, don't deluge visitors with financial information.

Traditionally, advisors see their website as an entry point, a selling opportunity and a resource for client education. For a Life-First Advisor the website is where prospects get a taste of the client experience. There is more emphasis on how the advisor's service makes the client *feel*.

Here are some things that will help you extend your brand through your website:

- An outline of your value proposition (using a lot of what you already have on your brochures).
- Links to other life-oriented sites.
- Articles on lifestyle and life transition issues.
- Links to some of your professional referral sources in the community.

Newsletters and email

Life-First Advisors can use their newsletters to position themselves as offering a holistic service to clients and as someone with access to a range of education resources and community experts.

The newsletter should be written to be *read*, which means it should be about clients' life concerns and provide them with entertaining and interesting perspectives. Content can come from other professionals and even from clients themselves.

Successful newsletters have professional production qualities and feature tight and colorful stories about real-life issues.

Quarterly publication works best, while the delivery method (digital or hard copy) depends on the age and connectivity of the clients.

For email updates to individual clients, content should be concise, timely and relevant. A client looking at putting a child through university might appreciate an article on tuition costs. Another considering a holiday in Nepal might welcome a travel piece from someone who trekked to Everest Base Camp.

In all of this communication, the focus should not be on selling but on delivering information of value and relevance.

Your communications strategy should focus on three constituencies:

- Clients with whom you already enjoy a relationship based on a good understanding of their personal concerns and a high level of trust.

- Clients with whom you aren't close, or where the relationship is based on a particular product or on your ability to facilitate a given transaction.

- Prospects who might be drawn to an advisor who offers life planning services and can give them some insight into elements of their lives.

Reinforce your brand

Client communication is not just a relationship management tool but also a marketing tool. So ensure you continue to reinforce your Life-First branding by:

Regularly sending non-financial information. You can't always be sure every client will read what you send but you never know what will strike a chord.

Suspending your own self-interest. Doing something for a client that doesn't relate to financial products tells them this is not a purely transactional relationship.

Staying top of mind. Life is unpredictable, so you should be clients' 'first call' after family when they need answers. Sharing life content reinforces that.

All of your communications should be right-brain focused by making an emotional connection. You can assist that effort by using client-friendly language that connects the dots while avoiding the acronyms, buzzwords and technical language prevalent in the financial services industry. The truth is jargon just makes you look like every other advisor and encourages clients to tune out.

Any reference to financial planning should be used in the context of helping the client reach their life goals.

A Life-First Advisor...

- Has a communications strategy that gives clients and prospects a real feel for their distinctive approach
- Maintains a store of good material on life planning issues to send to clients
- Makes good use of communications such as emails, mail-outs and newsletters to convey life planning information
- Offers a website rich in useful information and relevant links

11 | Educator of Choice

- **The Life-First Advisor pays more attention to client education than most other advisors**
- **Education is a key element of their value proposition**
- **Life-Planning Workshops reinforce your brand as an advisor interested in life issues, not just financial ones**

Industry studies show that clients have a thirst for education. When, in 2010, the Financial Planning Association asked US investors to name the services most valuable to them, education ranked as number one.

The Life-First Advisor pays more attention to client education than most other advisors — in fact, it's a key element of the Life-First Advisor's overall value proposition, covering self-discovery, clarity, insight and partnership.

Through your comprehensive and varied education program clients will be able to combine left-brain analysis and right-brain contemplation as they prepare for life transitions and the allied financial implications.

There are many ways to deliver education to your clients: personally or with the help of outside experts; through your client newsletter or in a workshop; via a computerized questionnaire or through the gift of a book.

Client education programs are important interactions between you and your client.

Education pieces

A simple way to show your clients you care about their life transitions
– but without requiring a one-to-one discussion just yet – is to have
education materials readily available, in 'hard copy' or online.

For a start, pamphlets, such as those shown here, can be displayed
in the waiting area of your office, where clients can browse through
them. These might address topics such as:

- Sending children to university.
- Becoming an empty nester.
- Preparing for retirement.
- Divorce.
- Long-term care options for loved ones.

Similar education pieces could be published on your website.

As well as providing useful information in a non-challenging way,
these education pieces reinforce your brand as a Life-First Advisor.

Education Pamphlets

Life Planning Workshops

Of the many tools Life-First Advisors use to deliver their messages to clients, the Life-Planning Workshop has proven to be the most effective.

If you could come up with a single tool to help you empower and motivate clients, draw new prospects in and reinforce your brand as a life planner, it would have all the attributes of the Life-Planning Workshop.

What better way to provide life-planning education than to get your clients and prospects in a room and give them a motivational, enthusiastic and insightful presentation on the keys to effectively planning the rest of their life?

That's the challenge, of course – for a Life-Planning Workshop to be effective it must offer all of those things. If it delivers anything less, it wastes the opportunity to position yourself as 'Life CFO'.

Some advisors are reluctant to take center stage. "There's no way I would ever want to get up in front of my clients and talk to them about how to plan their lives", one advisor said. "That's just not my nature and I'd appear insincere by attempting it". That same advisor, however, understood the advantages of conducting a Life-Planning Workshop, asking: "Is there some way I can do these workshops without actually having to do any of the presentation?"

Life-First Advisors should be prepared to offer workshops or seminars as part of their marketing plan. Education is, after all, what clients want. And as a Life-First Advisor you're saying your difference is the fact you work with clients to help them understand their lives, not just their money.

We're not asking you to plan their lives for them. But you do have a role in offering information on life, encouraging your clients to think about those issues and internalize a plan, then supporting those plans with your own and others' expertise.

Let's look at the four elements of an effective Life-Planning Workshop, where you will want to:

- Provide good quality information.
- Motivate attendees to take action.
- Empower them with tools .
- Stimulate their thinking.

Inform

You can easily access excellent information to pass on to clients on most aspects of life planning. But the question often asked is: "Do I have the right to pass on information to clients about things that are not relevant to financial advice?" Our answer is an emphatic yes, with a couple of caveats.

First, you should offer information only to those who want it, not force it on unwilling participants. So, as well as offering the best possible information, your workshops should be structured so clients can focus on areas of interest.

Be careful not to 'preach' or judge, and avoid sensitive topics such as spirituality and serious health issues such as alcoholism.

Second, think about how you deliver information that's outside your particular areas of expertise.

Recently, we spoke with a researcher in the gerontology department of a large university. Initially she questioned the credentials of a financial advisor to talk to clients about the aging process. When we explained that advisors wanted to learn about the key issues, from her studies, so they could share observations with clients, the gerontologist was more than happy to provide copies of her research.

You don't have to be the expert. You just have to know where the experts are and what the science is saying. Then you're entitled to share with clients some of the things you've discovered that may help them understand their own issues.

We've conducted hundreds of retirement lifestyle planning workshops without being a psychologist or gerontologist. Does that mean we have nothing to say? Far from it. In fact, you'll earn respect and gain credibility if you position yourself as a gatherer of information, rather than as the fount of all knowledge.

As we tell our audiences: *"The one thing I'm sure I'm an expert in is how to be someone in my early 50s trying to understand what's going on in my own life. Now, let me share with you some of the information I've been able to put together and perhaps together we can make some sense of it. Then you can take whatever is relevant to your own life and make it work for you."*

A bonus of using an outside expert is the possibility of inviting their clients to attend, widening your exposure to potential clients and giving them a chance to see how you are different.

Motivate

Get someone thinking about the issue that concerns them and you've cleared the major obstacle in motivating them. Advisors who feel they're not 'motivators' forget that motivation comes from within. The presenter and the workshop itself are catalysts, but it's the individuals in the audience who will take action if they can connect your information with their problem-solving need.

The workshop should provide opportunities for the audience to think about their own issues. Some of the best ways to do this are:

- Worksheet questionnaires that prompt participants to think.
- Discussion groups that encourage viewpoints to be shared.
- Goal-setting exercises that help couples, in particular, to agree on aims.
- Your personal stories, prompting participants to think about their own lives.
- Rhetorical questions, or questions to the audience, that invite discussion.

Your workshop should prepare fertile ground for whatever crop your audience needs to sow.

Empower

You can also provide some practical tools to help people build plans or address issues. Again, you're simply preparing fertile ground.

Earlier in this book we recalled the adage: 'People don't know what they don't know'. Your workshop should help participants understand the key issues in their lives by sharing the experiences of others who have gone through similar things.

You can also take the audience through a goal-setting process to help them organize their thoughts.

Stimulate

Are there common concerns you can address in an indirect way by simply putting some information out there? For example, if many members of your audience are aging baby boomers, is it safe to assume most have been thinking about their careers, their retirement outlook, their health and their relationships? How many of them have aging parents or 20-year-old children requiring assistance?

You've advertised a Life-Planning Workshop, so the people who attend can be expected to be thinking about life planning. The chances are good they've already thought a lot about the issues.

Focus their thoughts by letting them know in your advertising exactly what to expect. To ensure relevance, survey the room at the outset of the workshop to gauge expectations for the session.

Your opportunity

There are a number of roles for you at a Life-Planning Workshop, depending on the nature of the subject to be discussed and the expertise required.

One of the advantages of conducting these workshops is the opportunity to share your thoughts with participants. We urge you to try to participate in a meaningful way, even if your workshop uses outside experts as speakers.

For example, you could act as the master of ceremonies, introduce the speakers, moderate the question-and-answer session and sum up the presentations.

It would also be appropriate and effective to say a few words about the role you play in your client's life planning as a service of your practice. This is an opportunity to differentiate and brand yourself as a Life CFO. A few well-chosen (and non-sales or product-orientated) words can position you as a source of important information.

Try a Life-Planning Workshop. Many advisors who haven't conducted seminars before have found this approach to client education non-threatening, unique and a welcome change from the many financial seminars out there.

If you're reticent about talking to clients about certain life issues but believe there may be interest, the seminar is a simple way to identify those who do require further information.

Life-First Education opportunities

	Target Audience	Possible topics	Delivery	What's different?
General	Clients Prospects Referral networks	• Retirement lifestyle • Fit after Forty/Fifty • Healthy aging • Critical illness • Long-term health care • Children's education • Family budgeting • The internet • Second career • Non-financial keys to retirement success	• Newsletters • Website • Seminars • Articles • Pre-meeting package	• Life planning before financial planning • Emphasis on non-financial • Advisor as information conduit • Use of third-party sources • Use of outside experts • Client-centric not product-centric
Targeted Life Planning	Key clients Corporate prospects	• Life planning techniques • Employee life planning • Life transitions such as: • Career transition • Bereavement • Disability • Marriage & Divorce • Sudden wealth • Critical illness • Elder care • Retirement	• Forward articles • Send out books • Referrals to other professionals • General information sessions • Focused workshops	• Advisor as a coach • Advisor as 'human web browser' or source of non-financial information
Linked to Financial Planning	Key clients Clients Prospects Referral networks	• Sudden wealth • Suddenly single • Helping community • Gifts to loved ones • Saving for education • Saving for retirement • Low-stress investing • How markets affect your life' • Understanding your investment personality • Protecting loved ones • Targeted saving	• Newsletters • Website • Workshops • Seminars • Articles • Initial meeting with new clients • Regular meetings • Joint seminars with non-financial professionals	• All information framed in terms of life planning • Life planning as a branding tool

Let's look at the different types of Life-Planning Workshop, from large to small.

The Large Seminar

This type of event is aimed at attracting a large number of clients and prospects to hear a well-known speaker or to be educated on a given topic.

This sort of seminar went out of fashion for a while, but the life-based focus means this type of event is making a comeback. Today's aging baby boomer is seeking information on specific aspects of life planning, particularly in relation to health and retirement.

The keys to making a large seminar a success are:

Selling the speaker. The name doesn't always have to be well known – you can sell most names with a little work. But note that the less well known the name the harder you'll have to work.

Using your current clients as magnets to draw other people. If your topic is compelling and not financially oriented, your clients will be less shy about inviting another couple to join them. Again, the retirement lifestyle seminar has worked well in this regard.

Personal contact. The most successful seminars are those where you have worked the phones to let people know personally why they should attend. Remember that if you don't follow up on your initial approach you'll lose 50 percent of those who originally expressed interest.

Drip marketing. If you follow up your invitation with phone calls, letters and postcards marketing the event, as well as articles of interest surrounding the topic, you'll increase your audience.

Some examples of seminar topics that attract interest are:

- The high cost of education – helping children and grandchildren.
- Fit after 50.
- What you should know about caregiving.
- The 'snowbird' lifestyle – escaping to the sun.
- How to protect your lifestyle and your income.

- Conservative ways to protect your nest egg in retirement.
- How much does retirement really cost?
- Planning your life in retirement.
- Planning for your estate and your legacy.
- Turning success into significance.
- Building a charitable giving strategy.

The Small Client Workshop

These are less formal and can be held in your boardroom. The advantages are cost and intimacy. The disadvantage is smaller reach for your message. There are a number of different formats that can work well, which we look at below. Unlike the large seminar, you don't necessarily need a guest speaker, though this approach still works well at this level. Here are some ideas:

Coffee and Conversation
These sessions, aimed at retirees, can be conducted at a local restaurant before the lunch crowd arrives. The restaurant may give you a break on the cost of coffee and pastry simply because they see the potential to gain new customers.

Senior employee presentation
Companies often have a need – even a fiduciary responsibility – to provide information on their company pension plan or other retirement options. The topic of retirement lifestyle is of great interest to employees on the verge of retirement.

Specific demographic
Making a non-financial presentation to women's groups, seniors associations, service organizations and others is an effective way for advisors to gain exposure. It's a chance to extend your brand in the community.

Specific professional group
Professionals such as accountants and lawyers also advise clients on the future. Life-First Advisors can reach out to these groups to cover such topics as 'How to talk to clients about retirement' or 'The key issues facing the 50-plus client'.

Other outside groups

There's an old saying in the business: "Why spend time trying to get 50 people in a room when there are already rooms with 50 people in them?" Associations, trade groups and other organizations are always looking for speakers. Generally, financial planners aren't first on the list because of the perception they'll just try to sell something. Create a presentation on a topic of interest that doesn't attempt to 'sell' and you'll get in front of these groups.

Coffee and Conversation

Coffee and Conversation

Janet Thomas, ABC Financial
is pleased to present our special guest schedule for May

Wednesday May 1
June Messmer, General Manager, Hollyburn Seniors Lodge
What you should know about Senior's facilities for your loved ones

Wednesday May 8
Monika Hart, Nutritionist, Island Natural
How to keep healthy and happy after 50 – easy ways to diet and exercise for a busy lifestyle

Wednesday May 15
Bob Arnold, RCMP
Are you protecting your house, family and property effectively?

Wednesday May 22
Barbara Thomas, Psychologist
Important issues for women to consider if you are over 50 and on your own

Join us for coffee and conversation at The Table Restaurant, 10am-10:45am every Wednesday. Phone Donna Wilks 339-4704 to reserve your place.

The Life-First Advisor …

- Has a comprehensive education program for clients focusing on life transitions
- Creates a relationship with other professionals in their community who can help educate clients
- Keeps the education focus on life issues, not just financial issues

12 | But Women *are* Different

- Evidence suggests that Men and women tend to look at money in different ways
- Life-First Advisors focus their advice to women on issues such as family and lifestyle
- Objectives-based planning resonates with female clients

"Why is the women's market any different?" the marketing manager of an investment firm asked. "If I were a woman, I'd be offended by an approach that suggested my needs differ from a man's." We don't intend to "over-generalize" or make sexist assumptions that don't hold up in evidence.

The Life-First Approach works well with *both* men and women – but it's an absolute necessity if you're to establish your relevance to the women's market.

While it's true some women clients do feel a program geared to them somehow denigrates them, the fact is that women do have different needs and, generally, respond to a different approach. The Life-First Approach, which recognizes the role emotion plays in a client's decision-making, will resonate well with women clients and prospects as well as many men.

Many of your women clients will say to you that investment management and financial planning don't have a gender. They'd be right. Men don't have a corner on the need for quality investment management and both men and women are actively involved in financial planning for their families. Not all women need financial education and it's unfair to generalize by saying men normally handle the finances.

Both men and women need your advice and expertise. However, there are some areas where the Life-First Approach is particularly relevant for women.

Equal but different

Most women wouldn't want to be treated any differently to a man. But that doesn't mean you shouldn't focus part of your service offering on some of the major issues for women:

Women live longer. Women now outlive men by an average of seven years. This means they have to save more because they'll have more years of retirement to fund. Women represent around half of the population. But, in the US, they represent 53 percent of the population aged 65-74, some 60 percent of the 74-85 cohort and 70 percent of the population aged over 85. In fact, 80 percent of America's centenarians are women.[15]

This is a maturing marketplace and it will be dominated by women. Women are becoming major consumers of financial services and key decision makers. A major American investment house found that while their average client was 58 and more likely to be male, among clients over the age of 75 some 68 percent were women. Women also drive a considerable percentage of consumer purchased. For example, in Australia this number is estimated at over 80%![16]

Women tend to be the main caregiver for elderly parents. Your discussion of caregiving and managing parental assets will affect both male and female clients but will likely find a more interested audience among women.

[15] US Census Information 2012
[16] A.T.Kearney, Consulting, 2013

Women tend to have longer retirements. Both men and women need help preparing for a long retirement, but women need even more help to handle the extra years they live. In addition, research shows that many women enter this period of life with fewer resources than men of the same age.

Women are more likely to live alone in retirement. Issues such as household budgeting, health care, financial planning, legacy issues and investment management increasingly will be taken on by single, elder women who may not be aware of some of the financial consequences of some life issues.

Women are taking a more active role in family finances. Increasingly, women – professionals and caregivers – are taking control of the family finances. According to the National Center for Women and Retirement Research in New York, 80 percent to 90 percent of all women in the United States today will be the sole decision maker in their family finances at some point. This could be one of the biggest shifts in financial advice of the next few decades.

Women tend to earn and save less over their lifetimes. There's plenty of data on the wages gap between men and women, something that's compounded by women having career breaks to raise children – affecting lifetime income and their ability to accumulate pension or superannuation credits. Other research points to the savings rate for women being half that for men. The issue of retirement planning takes on particular urgency if there are insufficient funds to finance it. Is that a gender issue? Not entirely, but it's certainly a major issue many women will have to face.

Women avoid making investment decisions. According to Dreyfus Corporation and the National Center for Women and Retirement Research, women are 50 percent more likely than men to avoid making investment decisions for fear of making a mistake. Generally, women are more conservative investors than men, according to this research. Reduced returns from 'safe' investments could jeopardize their ability to meet retirement plan objectives.

Do all women – and their advisors – understand these undercurrents? Probably not. Many women take the same view of financial planning and investment planning as men but the issues above are not gender neutral and require a special approach.

Women need to be alerted to the important issues they'll face in the future. Once they recognize the different challenges they face they'll expect focused advice from someone who understands their life-based issues.

What women want

So what do women want from their money? The Employee Benefit Research Institute Retirement Confidence Survey of 2012 asked US women to name their top financial goals. Another study by the American Institute for Elder Planning Studies came up with similar results. Here's what they found to be the top concerns:

Women want to feel safe. Safety and freedom from fear consistently appeared in the responses. Safety can be defined in a number of ways, and many advisors might assume there's a link to conservative or guaranteed investments. In fact, safety refers more to a life free from worry or upset.

Advisors need to be aware that men and women don't always look at risk in the same way. Risk for a man usually equates with price volatility – the risk their investment will go down in value. But the risk women focus on, in general, is the risk they won't be able to maintain their lifestyle, because of that falling investment.

So, your focus when broaching subjects such as risk, investment performance and financial solutions should be on the relationship to lifestyle. A poor return from a mutual fund this month won't necessarily challenge the client's security. Remind them the investment strategies, insurance policies and tax planning that are in place all work towards creating long-term safety and financial comfort.

Women want to feel in control of quality of life. A big concern for women is losing the quality of life they currently enjoy. In fact, one of the biggest concerns in divorce is the potential threat to lifestyle from becoming single. Other potential threats to lifestyle include bereavement, retirement, job loss, education costs, health challenges and caregiving for an elder parent. These are all emotional 'hot buttons' that serve as reasons to develop a financial strategy.

In developing plans, a man might like an investment because the fund is a top-quartile performer or a critical illness policy because it provides $250,000 in coverage for just $160 a month. A woman, on the other hand, is likely to consider what the investment or insurance policy will mean to maintaining her quality of life in the long term.

Women want a comfortable standard of living in retirement. Many women are realistic when it comes to life in retirement. From an actuarial perspective, women are likely to survive their spouses in retirement. In fact, 90 percent of all US women will be the sole financial decision maker in their family at some point in their retirement.

Retirement lifestyle planning is an approach that resonates well with women. Not only are the lifestyle aspects discussed but also the unique financial considerations. Women will likely have a much longer retirement than men. As a result, the relationship between financial comfort and longevity is an important one to address.

Gender marketing

Successful marketing to women recognizes the strong role emotion plays in their decision-making. A woman's view of her role in family issues, her concern about her own independence in the future, her relationships to friends and community are among the things that must be taken into consideration in order to send a marketing message that she will find relevant.

Here are six keys to successful marketing to women:

Women are generally more risk-averse. As nurturers, they're concerned with protecting their loved ones. Targeted marketing has to focus on providing safety and be relevant to lifestyle in order to overcome aversion to risk.

Working women are sensitive to time pressure. Marketing should show them how a solution will make their lives easier and help them manage time. Women have more money today but less time. As a result they're more likely to seek out a professional advisor than a man. In a recent survey conducted by the US's largest insurer, 40 percent of women surveyed said they would seek retirement advice from an advisor versus just 25 percent of men.

Campaigns that educate, empower and reassure resonate with women. The opportunity for the financial services marketer is to help women create better lives for themselves by optimizing their financial resources.

'One size fits all' doesn't work. Life stage marketing, which recognizes the challenges that arise at each life transition are far more effective than campaigns suggesting all women need investment education or all women want to stop working, by way of example.

Women respond to the right-brain approach. Emotional attachment to your message is the key element in reaching the women's market. All approaches should clearly relate the benefit of your message to life issues.

Women won't buy something they neither want nor need. An aggressive or product-oriented approach will likely miss the mark with most women. Don't take the 'if I build it, they will come' approach. Beware a tone in seminars that says, 'I know what's good for you' or 'I'm smarter than you'. And it's not enough to be a woman advisor marketing to women. Unless you help women understand the life need that will be met by your product or solution, and empower women to make decisions for themselves, you're wasting your time.

Advisor as educator

The Life-First Approach is to educate clients on how you can help them feel better about their emotional challenges and the financial decisions they need to make.

There are two elements to educating women clients that you should consider:

- What is the overall level of investment knowledge my client has?
- What are their emotional life issues that have financial implications?

Managing Your Money Workshop

Managing Your Money
Financial Empowerment for Today's Woman

You are invited..

Attend this special workshop, presented by Barbara Smith, Fincancial Advisor, ABC Financial.

Thursday - April 11 - 2017 at 11:30 AM
Call for details & reservations at 888.555.1234

If you're like many of Barbara's active women clients, you are faced with the challenged of balancing your life with the demands of making your money work for you.

This workshop has been designed with you in mind.

Today's baby boomer woman investor is likely to have a post-secondary education and be very aware of investment issues. However, there will still be clients who have left investment decisions to their partner.

As part of your discovery process, you should have a conversation (not an inquisition) about their views on:

- Budgeting.
- The stock market.
- Interest rates.
- Insurance and its role.
- Pensions and retirement programs.
- Long-term care protection.
- Children's or grandchildren's education.

Try to get a sense of how much time your client has spent thinking about these issues and areas where they may welcome your education.

Many education programs for women miss the mark because they focus on investing basics. These 'investing for women' seminars teach the basics of mutual funds, insurance and how the stock market works. "What's the problem?' you might ask. "Both women and men should take every opportunity to learn about investment basics and besides, women are less educated on these than men."

Of course, not all women are less informed. And education should not only cover the basics but also address key emotional issues where a financial planning solution would help. So your education program should start with those life planning concerns and then tie the financial education program to them.

Creative educational opportunities

Advisors have identified a number of target markets among women for their education efforts. Here are a few:

Women entrepreneurs. Did you know that in the US the number of self-employed women is growing at a much faster rate than self-employed men? Today 12 percent of women in the workforce fall into this category. Why not bring in a small business expert, career transition specialist or tax accountant for a joint workshop?

Affluent women. These women are much more likely to be altruistic than their male counterparts. Philanthropy is a good theme to use in this market and there are a number of experts in your community whose expertise and networks you can leverage.

Elder care givers. Seminars on caregiving for the daughters of aging parents can be held in conjunction with a long-term care provider or with professional caregivers. Look out for clients who have parents who may require care in the future, and those whose parent has recently lost their partner.

Employee groups. Luncheon workshops are a great idea for employees of local businesses. Contact the HR department and offer to talk to a group of their older women employees about pension or retirement issues. This segment may include lower-income earners who can't take advantage of all your services, but you never know when a future client will be sitting in the room. At the very least, you're providing a valuable service to senior management of the business.

Here are some ideas for education programs aimed at women:

- Managing life on your own.
- Taking control – the women's financial empowerment workshop.
- Caregiving and the people you care about.
- Suddenly single – what you need to know about the financial side of divorce.
- Fit after fifty – what every woman needs to know.
- Helping your spouse deal with retirement.
- Creating a legacy – helping your children and grandchildren.
- Creating your own vision of retirement – a woman's workshop.

Remember, your prospective audience must feel the information is aimed specifically at *them*.

The education should be presented by a speaker who has an understanding of women's issues. And your seminar should be clearly titled to create an emotional response, letting your audience know how the seminar will benefit their life rather than their money.

Invitation – For Today's Active Woman

For Today's Active Woman
Helping **You** relate **Your** money to **Your** Life.

Prospecting for change

The Life-First Approach to financial planning is a life-transition approach. Life changes such as divorce, an empty nest, retirement and bereavement have tremendous financial, psychological and emotional effects on men and women.

However, there's a growing trend among women to use these life events as an opportunity to 'take back' the power they may feel they relinquished in their lives. Your role as their advisor is to be both an educator and a catalyst.

Many advisors are not aware their clients are undergoing a painful life transition. This is particularly true if the discovery process doesn't go deep and the relationship has been based on financial planning or investment issues only.

But some advisors are now actively 'prospecting' for change, finding ways to identify clients who might need help.

Obviously, changing your discovery process so that it actively identifies potential life changes is an important step.

Another way to do this is to create a seminar or workshop that focuses on a life change of importance to women, such as divorce, empty nesting or bereavement. Each of the life issues in the table below is a potential workshop. Wherever possible, use female presenters and facilitators. The women who attend could be signaling they need further assistance.

You can also work with other experts who counsel clients undergoing change, making yourself available for referral to help their clients understand the financial consequences of the life event.

Let's look at some of the key life transitions that affect women, along with some of the potential financial consequences:

Key Life Transitions for Women

Life Transition	Emotional issues	Financial concerns
Marriage	<ul><li>Compromise independence</li><li>Relationship challenges</li><li>Shared responsibilities</li><li>Building a home life</li><li>Health concerns for spouse</li></ul>	<ul><li>Sharing financial decisions</li><li>Changing financial goals</li><li>Protection for family and future</li><li>Establish financial comfort</li><li>Maintaining lifestyle</li></ul>
Children	<ul><li>Caregiving and nurturing</li><li>Education</li><li>Changes in self-image</li></ul>	<ul><li>Family budgeting</li><li>Children's financial needs</li><li>Long-term education planning</li><li>Protecting lifestyle</li></ul>
Divorce	<ul><li>Single parenting</li><li>Change in lifestyle</li><li>Personal goal setting</li></ul>	<ul><li>Family or personal budgeting</li><li>Change in income</li><li>Increase/decrease in assets</li><li>Change in retirement plan</li><li>Insurance considerations</li><li>Pension plan understanding</li></ul>
Empty Nest	<ul><li>Change in lifestyle</li><li>Change in residence</li><li>Emotional loss</li></ul>	<ul><li>Living expenses</li><li>Change in financial plan</li></ul>
Retirement	<ul><li>Change in relationships</li><li>Change in lifestyle</li><li>Develop new goals</li></ul>	<ul><li>Change in family budget and income</li><li>Legacy issues</li><li>Financing dreams and goals</li></ul>
Health challenge	<ul><li>Changes in outlook</li><li>Need for caregiving</li><li>Change in relationship dynamic</li></ul>	<ul><li>Care costs</li><li>Change in family budget</li></ul>
Bereavement	<ul><li>Emotional loss</li><li>New responsibilities</li><li>Change in self-image</li><li>Change in family dynamic</li><li>Adjust to new lifestyle</li><li>Residence change</li></ul>	<ul><li>Financial education</li><li>Financial reorganization</li><li>Estate settlement</li><li>Change in financial plans</li><li>Change in family budgeting</li><li>Income changes</li></ul>
Residence change	<ul><li>Emotional loss</li><li>New lifestyle</li><li>Downsizing issues</li><li>Family proximity</li></ul>	<ul><li>Real estate buy and sell</li><li>Change in family budgeting</li></ul>
Loss of independence	<ul><li>Change in self-image</li><li>Change in residence</li><li>Need for caregiving</li></ul>	<ul><li>Share or give up financial management</li><li>Estate issues</li></ul>

Many of your women clients and prospects may be facing these issues for the first time. Your opportunity is to provide them with a comfortable space to talk about the emotional aspects of life change. Remember that issues are emotional before they become financial.

Networking opportunities

Faith Popcorn has a concept she calls 'think link'. Popcorn says that, "Brands must be differentiated not in the way you bring the components together but in the way you bring women together". This is one of the least understood and yet the most important reasons for marketing specifically to women's groups.

There are many common issues that will bring women together. Look no further than the success of investment clubs, book clubs and 'party' marketing to see the attraction 'think links' have.

Women form close emotional relationships with family, friends and colleagues. The advisor who focuses on the women's market recognizes there will be additional opportunities as long as they position themselves as the advisor of choice with their women clients.

The Life-First Advisor …

- Understands the different ways men and women tend to approach financial issues
- Considers the retirement life needs of single women and how to partner with them as coach and advisor
- Becomes an educator in the women's market with relevant workshops
- Appreciates the networks that women build

13 | Family Issues

- **Family issues are high in emotion and can have large financial implications**
- **It's important to understand clients' values and beliefs around family and money**
- **A particularly important discussion is the one around long-term care**

Discussions about family issues generally evoke the strongest emotional response of any planning issue. Whether it involves protecting a spouse, meeting the needs of children or helping aging parents, family is likely to be one of the strongest drivers for making financial plans.

The inter-generational transfer of wealth within families is one of the greatest challenges facing advisors today – both in terms of guiding families through this but also because of the implications for their own businesses. Many advisors have watched a large portfolio leave when the male client dies and his widow moves to another advisor.

In the next two decades trillions of dollars will flow from parents to children and grandchildren around the world.

It's clear that family issues ranging from educating children through to long-term care for elderly parents can be both emotional and impactful financially. It's an area where an advisor must tread, but tread carefully – understanding that people hold different values and beliefs around family and money.

Elder care

According to Ken Dychtwald, author of *Age Wave*, 70 percent of baby boomer households have not had a detailed discussion with their parents about the elders' financial situation.

From a financial planning perspective, this represents a huge void for the advisor when it comes to understanding some of the future obligations and emotional concerns of his or her boomer clients. [17]

Perhaps one of the biggest issues is the potential need for long-term care for parents, if not yourself further down the track. Some 43 percent of Americans aged over 65 will, at some point, live in a nursing home or long-term care facility. Of those, 10 percent will stay in a nursing home for five years or more.

For those who remain at home, care often will be provided by an adult daughter. It remains true today that women are the main caregivers for elder parents. It has been estimated that the average American women will spend 17 years raising a child, then 18 years looking after an elderly parent. In fact, a US government study found the top reason for absenteeism among women aged over 45 was caring for aging parents – and paid or unpaid in-home care is the way of the future, which will have implications for a family's time and financial resources.

The odds are that you, too, will need long-term care at some point[18].

- At age 55, the odds are 1 in 10.
- At age 65, the odds are 4 in 10.
- At age 75, the odds are 6 in 10.
- Past age 75, the odds are 7 in 10.

---

[17] Dychtwald and Flower, *The Age Wave*, 1989, revised
[18] Sun Life, 2015

This is both an emotional and financial risk for clients and their immediate families, as made plain by the table of indicative costs below.

Long-term care cost analysis

Leading causes of long-term care	Average length of care	Total cost of private room @$200/day	Total cost of semi-private @$170/day
Alzheimer's	96 months	$576,000	$489,000
Cancer	36 months	$216,000	$183,600
Cardiac	16 months	$96,000	$81,000
Diabetes	48 months	$288,000	$244,000
Pulmonary	36 months	$216,000	$183,000
Stroke	21 months	$126,000	$107,100

Source: US Center for Disease Control and AARP, 2015

In the US, Medicare doesn't usually pay for 'residential'-type expenses and Medicaid payments only kick in upon the depletion of the elder's assets. Provincial Health Plans cover only a portion of the costs. In addition, with a few exceptions, private medical insurance in Canada, the US, New Zealand and Australia does not cover long-term age care.

The long-term care discussion

Long-term care is therefore not a discussion an advisor can ignore and it should be tackled on two fronts, covering both the client themselves and their elder parents.

Advisors should talk about long-term care insurance and critical illness insurance as it benefits the client and spouse or partner. They should then expand the discussion to include elder parents and their situation. In both cases, the advisor is assessing the risks to the client's financial plan and identifying potential sources of income to fund long-term care. Many advisors are uncomfortable with this discussion, particularly when it comes to talking about aging parents. For an investment-oriented advisor, long-term care is not part of the picture when it comes to managing a client's nest egg.

However, long-term care represents a huge emotional and financial risk and is one the client seldom appreciates.

Does the advisor have the right to enquire as to the health of parents? Absolutely! After all, *any* potential risk to the client's plans has to be assessed and accounted for. You could start by asking these questions:

'To understand your situation, I want to gain a better understanding of your family. Tell me about your siblings. Are your parents still alive?' You are delicately bringing up the subject of whether the client's (or spouse's) parents are still alive and active, while explaining why you need this information. Learning more about siblings will give you a better idea of who else might be involved in caregiving and who has a potential interest in the parents' affairs.

'Where do they live?' This will give you an idea of how regularly the client sees their parents and whether there's already some caregiving taking place. It will also give you a chance, at another time, to ascertain where the parents' assets are and who is advising them.

'Are they in good health?' This is an opportunity to compare notes on your own parents or in-laws – sharing your personal story – while assessing the immediate or potential needs for caregiving.

'Have they looked after themselves financially?' Touchy question, but necessary. You want to understand whether they can look after themselves in the future, as well as opportunities to provide your expertise.

'Do you see a time when you may have to look after them, financially or otherwise?' Again, you are assessing risk while also showing your client you are being thorough in understanding the risks associated with long-term care issues. This question will help you understand some of the timing issues.

The discussion should uncover to what extent the client is aware of long-term care issues and what the potential needs may be of the people for whom they may be financially or emotionally responsible.

The discovery process should have raised some of this, but the long-term care discussion can reveal the specific risks associated with each person and lead to the gathering of details such as medical history.

The key questions are what kind of financial resources are available to fund future long-term care needs and what, ultimately, will be the client's responsibility?

Supporting the next generation

Let's face it – higher education is crucial to the success of our children and grandchildren. On average, graduates with a bachelor's degree earn 62 percent more a year than high school graduates. A 2011 study found that, on average, US graduates with a bachelor's degree earn 84 percent more per year than high school graduates. [19] Clearly, one of the best investments you can make for your children or grandchildren is the investment in their education.

---

[19] Georgetown University, Center on Education and the Workforce, 2011

Yet, many advisors don't talk to clients about this, simply because the numbers don't add up for them. Education investment plans in the US and Canada tend to be small investments. In most US states a 529 account can't exceed $250,000, and most never approach that. In Canada, a Registered Education Savings Plan has a maximum yearly contribution of $2000, hardly the kind of investment to spark the interest of most advisors.

Yet the costs of education are skyrocketing. In Australia, for example, the education inflation index has risen 5.7 percent a year over the last 20 years, outpacing much lower general inflation. With governments around the world tightening their belts, individuals can expect to pick up more of the tab for education in those places where it is currently subsidized.

This makes the education discussion, with clients who are parents or grandparents, an important one as a life need with potentially large financial ramifications.

A family approach to Discovery

The Life-First Discovery process is the time to start asking clients about family. The goal is to identify issues or opportunities where you can add value. Here's our three-step process for 'getting to know' a client's family.

Step 1 – Build trust and rapport

When meeting new clients usually the first challenge is to build rapport and comfort. Conversation about family is an easy way to break the ice – there are few things that are more likely to produce an emotional connection. Here are some discussion 'openers'. One tip: make sure you reflect the client's own words in your note taking.

Breaking the ice...

QUESTION	PURPOSE
▪ Tell me about your family	▪ This gets the client talking about the people in their lives who are important to them. This also gives you a chance to share information on your family and to find common ground.
▪ Do you have children or grandchildren? ▪ How old are they? ▪ Boys or girls?	▪ This is an alternative question or simply an expansion of the first question. You will go into this deeper in the discovery phase, but for now you simply want to create a conversation about a comfortable subject.
▪ Where are you from?	▪ Not 'where do you live?' but 'where did you grow up?' This gives you an idea of values that may have influenced your client in their early years. Did they grow up on a farm, in a small town or in a big city?
▪ Do you come from a big family?	▪ This opens a discussion on siblings that will give you an idea of where brothers and sisters are and what they do.
▪ Are your parents still alive? ▪ Where do they live? ▪ Are they still in good health?	▪ This gives you an idea of the potential for caregiving, inheritance or other emotional demands. Tip: Don't make this sound like a fact finder. You're simply showing interest in the parents, and you can share information about your own as a way to build rapport.

Conventional wisdom says you should always ask open-ended questions but we don't think that's the case at this stage of the conversation: initial questions that produce short answers allow you to follow up with other questions or to share your own personal story. Remember, this is about give and take, not just an opportunity for you to ask and the client to answer.

Step 2 – Identify values and beliefs

It's important to understand the values and beliefs your client attaches to family and wealth. Start with some general questions then follow up with more focused questions to enhance your understanding.

Start by setting the stage: *"Mrs Smith, as we build a long-term plan for you and your family, it's really important for us to consider all the issues that might concern you in the future. For most of us, the number one consideration in a financial plan is to look after our families. I'd like to take a few minutes to get to know more about your family and what's important to you about planning for them".*

Exploring Values and Beliefs

QUESTION	PURPOSE
■ What were some of the most important lessons about money you were taught by your parents?	■ This gives you a clue to your client's attitude towards money. It also indicates how the parents handled money and potentially how the client's children might view money.
■ Who is directly affected by the financial decisions you make?	■ You want an idea of the family members who are most important to the client. This could go beyond immediate family and include parents, siblings and adult children, for example.
■ Have your parents looked after themselves financially?	■ You are establishing potential sources of concern for the client as well as gaining a better understanding of possible inheritance issues.
■ Tell me about the family you have who live close by	■ You will get a good idea of what family members are close by who could be part of any contingency plan in case something happens to your client.
■ Is there a possibility you may be called upon to use your assets to help someone in your family?	■ This opens the door to talking about parents or children who may be struggling.
■ How do you feel about your ability to help your family?	■ You want to establish whether the client wants to help. Some don't, while others haven't even thought about it. This is your chance to explore the family values involved.
■ What kinds of things do you want to do to create more lifestyle enjoyment for your family?	■ This touches on future plans such as holidays and other leisure activities.
■ What life changes in your family will directly affect your financial plan in the future?	■ It is important to consider what kinds of family life transitions they may encounter in the future.
■ How comfortable are you about your retirement plans today?	■ Many people haven't really worked out their retirement plan and haven't even talked about their plans with their spouse. This will give you the opportunity to open the retirement conversation.

Step 3 – Identify opportunities

Answers to some of the questions you ask will suggest follow-up inquiries to help you identify opportunities to provide value.

What's next?

QUESTION	FOLLOW-UP QUESTION	OPPORTUNITY
■ Tell me about your children and grandchildren. ■ How old are they? ■ What grades are they in at school? ■ How important is education funding in your financial plan? ■ Are you concerned about how they will fund their education? ■ What plans are in place to look after their education?	■ What are their plans for the future? ■ Have you thought about how expensive education might be in the future? ■ Are there roadblocks that might affect your children's (grandchildren's) future education plans? ■ What protection do you have in place in case anything happens to you?	■ Solution that addresses the educational needs of your client's children or grandchildren
■ How much do your children understand your financial situation today? ■ What is the most important lesson you can give your children today about money? ■ Where do your children go when they need financial advice? ■ Are there some things we can do today to educate your children on financial issues so it will be easier on them in the future?	■ What concerns do you have about your children's future? ■ Is there anything we can do today to help them in the future?	■ Educating children and other family members
■ What plans do you have in place to pass on your assets to your family if anything were to happen to you? ■ Have you discussed all of your financial issues with your spouse? ■ Are you in agreement regarding how you have laid things out in your estate plan? ■ When was the last time you updated your Will? ■ Have you thought about how you can help your family today rather than waiting until you aren't here? ■ What plans do you have in place to look after your children from your first marriage?	■ What is it that you want your money to do for your family in the future? ■ What do you see as the biggest threat to your family's lifestyle in the future? ■ What plans do you have in place to protect them? ■ What problems might arise for your family when they administer your estate? ■ Could there be challenges when your Will is probated? ■ If we were to look at some ways to use your assets today to help your children, what effect would that have on their future? ■ What are your plans regarding your holiday home should anything happen to you?	■ Creating a Will and Estate Plan

▪ How involved is your family in your business today? ▪ Who in your family is affected by the business decisions you make? ▪ How have you protected your family should anything happen to your business?	▪ What are your plans regarding your business if something happens to you? ▪ What concerns do you have about the success of your business in the future? ▪ What is the biggest threat to your business? ▪ What are your plans for your business?	▪ Creating a plan for passing on the ownership of a family business
▪ What have your parents set up in their Will to pass on their assets to their family? Have you talked to your parents about how they want their affairs handled if they are no longer able to do it for themselves? ▪ Are you comfortable that your parents are managing their financial affairs properly today? ▪ Who currently advises your parents on their financial affairs? ▪ How active are you in advising them? ▪ Have you thought about your parents potentially needing caregiving?	▪ Do you feel you'll have to be more involved in your parents' affairs in the future? ▪ How might your parents' financial concerns affect your financial plan? ▪ At what point do you feel your parents will no longer be able to live independently? ▪ Will your parents have sufficient resources if they need long-term care? ▪ What would happen to your parents' estate if they were to encounter a serious health challenge? ▪ What will be your biggest challenge when your parents pass on?	▪ Setting up Will and Estate Plans for elderly parents, as well as provisions for Power of Attorney
▪ What is your biggest concern right now regarding your financial situation? ▪ How much do you understand about your current situation? ▪ Who else can give you some guidance and support regarding your financial situation? ▪ How supportive is your family when it comes to organizing your financial affairs?	▪ What concerns do you have about the future? ▪ What kind of help will you need in the future to manage your financial affairs? ▪ How do you see your lifestyle changing in the future?	▪ Solutions for a newly widowed client (Be careful – there is a big difference between a conversation with a recently bereaved client and one who has had time to process a loss.)

By the end of this process you should have a good grasp of your client's family situation and the potential for family to produce life issues with serious financial implications. Knowing their values and beliefs around family and money, you will be better placed to help clients develop solutions that address their needs in a way they're comfortable with as parents, partners and caregivers.

The Life-First Advisor ...

- Positions their value in terms of how they can help family
- Tries to build intergenerational relationships, perhaps using the concept of the 'Family Office' to promote planning issues around family
- Ensures they understand the important issues to do with a client's estate plan, including powers of attorney and final instructions

14 | The Life-First Retirement Advisor

- **Retirement life planning is not just about wealth but also about health and happiness**
- **Clients are looking for a new kind of retirement**
- **The ideal retirement 'personality' has four key attributes**

"Just once I would like to have a discussion with my financial advisor that showed he really understood me!" Tom says. "While I don't expect him to be an expert on retirement, I'd at least like to feel he has put together a plan that fits my life."

Tom is on the verge of retirement from his job as a sales manager at a major manufacturing firm. He will be 60 next year. Tom feels he is finally in a position to walk away from his job and to start enjoying life with his wife Margaret. They have been dreaming about their retirement and have already made plans to become 'snowbirds' who follow the sun.

Tom's frustration comes from the fact his financial advisor hasn't ever asked him about what he plans to do. "I finally had to ask him if maybe Margaret should come into the office and sit down with him also," Tom says. "My advisor has never met my wife, even though we have a joint account."

That's not to say Tom and Margaret's financial advisor hasn't done a fine job for them in the past 15 years. In fact, the advisor has made some good recommendations over time and has them in reasonable financial shape on the eve of their retirement. Their retirement savings have continued to grow and, combined with the work pensions both will receive, should provide a nice retirement income.

"Where we really need the help now," says Margaret, "is in understanding just what we should be planning for in the future. Maybe that isn't what a financial advisor is supposed to do, but I don't know who else would be able to give us a heads up on the financial considerations we should think about in retirement."

Like many, Tom and Margaret are entering retirement without a clear understanding of this next phase of life. Intuitively they recognize their life will change over time, but they are uncertain about how those changes will affect their financial plan or vice versa. They do recognize, however, that they will require a different kind of discussion with their financial advisor than simply setting an accumulation target and then measuring against it on a regular basis.

"One of the things I really don't know," says Tom, "is how much is retirement going to cost? My advisor says we will have more than enough money so we really shouldn't worry, but I like to feel like I have a handle on things."

Although Tom and Margaret can calculate how much they spend now, and then try to figure out how that will change over time, they're left with the feeling a retirement financial plan has to start with lifestyle issues first. It isn't just about numbers any more if it's going to be relevant to their goals for the future.

"I guess that's where the disconnect comes with our advisor," sighs Margaret. "I don't know how our advisor can possibly create a financial plan for retirement without even asking us about how we want to live it."

More than money

One of the most obvious life transitions your clients will face is retirement. As the aging baby boomer begins to look at retirement in real terms rather than as a long-term financial planning exercise, the advisor will be called upon to provide relevant education, solutions and services.

For many advisors and their clients, retirement has been a financial and product issue so far. In fact, much of the growth of the financial services industry has been fostered by the need for aging boomers to save for retirement. Retirement planning is treated as almost interchangeable with investment planning and very little work has been done on educating clients on the non-financial aspects of this next phase of life.

That shouldn't be a surprise. After all, Life-First retirement lifestyle planning goes far beyond financial planning and calls on the advisor to consider areas outside investment and product.

Barry recently received an invitation as part of a mail drop to attend a retirement lifestyle seminar, put on by a local investment advisor in the town where he lives. Out of curiosity, he contacted the advisor to find out what the seminar would cover.

"We'll cover all of the major areas", the advisor said. "I'm going to focus on income options in retirement, on how to invest in retirement and what you need to know about payout options. In addition, we'll cover various asset allocation strategies that retirees can use. Finally, I'm going to introduce a new retirement product that will make your life easier."

Barry asked whether the seminar would cover such things as fulfilling activities in retirement, or the effect retirement has on relationships or maybe healthy ageing?

The advisor responded that he was a financial advisor and didn't want to get into those issues. When Barry asked where the retirement lifestyle planning part came in, the advisor said it was up to clients to take the financial advice and then work out the lifestyle issues on their own.

Does the advisor have any place discussing retirement lifestyle planning issues? It depends on the expertise of the advisor and the relationship with the client.

Ultimately, a sound financial plan for retirement can't really be designed unless the client has a clear view of what his or her retirement is going to look like. As one Life-First Advisor says below, the problem is most clients are clear on what they are retiring *from* but not so clear on what they are retiring *to.*

Retirement lifestyle planning is a great opportunity for the advisor to bring in experts to talk about specific issues. In fact, many of the issues we discuss in this chapter would be best addressed with the help of other professionals. There will be a ready audience for workshops and seminars on these topics, as people seek clarity.

The Life-First Advisors who actively conduct retirement lifestyle planning seminars take programs to their clients but also to employee groups, associations, unions, community colleges and corporations. They enlist the assistance of professionals including:

- Psychologists.
- Fitness instructors.
- Career transition experts.
- Personal coaches.
- Doctors.
- Travel agents.
- Gerontologists.
- Age care specialists.

Go back to our chapter on the advisor as Educator of Choice for a reminder of what's involved in this sort of seminar.

Redefining retirement

According to the American Association of Retired Persons (AARP), 85 percent of today's baby boomers expect to work when they retire from their present jobs. That means just 15 percent of baby boomers are looking at a traditional retirement – no work and 25 years or more of prolonged leisure.

It's likely the word retirement as we know it will *not exist* within a generation.

One of the important roles for the advisor, then, is to help clients clarify what they really want their retirement to look like – as opposed to the 'retirement dream' they see in advertising. An advisor may be making incorrect assumptions about what a client plans, and the client may be unclear about what the advisor is helping them plan for.

Between them, they can consider whether:

- The client may not actually want to retire, at least not now.

- The client may want to start their own business.

- The client may want some form of staged retirement.

- The client may want to switch careers and do something in keeping with their skills and interests.

- The client may want to try traditional retirement for a while and then make a decision on whether this will be permanent

All of these are options in today's retirement. The advisor should find ways to create 'fertile ground' in the client's mind so they can fill in their personal picture of retirement.

There are some questions the advisor should ask to help the client clarify their retirement vision – starting with when they plan to retire but also questions that will draw out what they see themselves doing in areas such as work, business, family, leisure and education. How well prepared do they feel? What are their greatest concerns?

In the appendices, we provide a worksheet you can use as a foundation for discussion.

Second Life

Retirement is as much a psychological issue as it is a financial or workplace one. This life phase will bring its share of challenges and the advisor will often be in a position to help the client understand the financial consequences of those challenges. Here's how one Life-First Advisor presents the opportunities in retirement ...

'The Japanese have an interesting approach to the retirement phase of their life. Rather than using the word 'retirement' to define the final stage of life, Japanese society has the concept of 'Second Life'. This is the period of time in your life when your family responsibilities have changed and you can focus on your 'inner peace'. It is a time when you get closer to your soul and dispense your wisdom to benefit younger generations.

This next phase of your life gives you the opportunity to:

- **Find life meaning rather than 'resting'.** This next phase of life gives people the opportunity to tie their life plan more closely to the values and life goals they may have had but didn't have the time for while working.

- **Achieve life balance over lopsided leisure**. While retirement for some is one long weekend, your retirement can be a fulfilling combination of quality leisure, satisfying work and the pursuit of self-knowledge.

- **Realize lifelong dreams over time-filling fun**. Goal setting can be a fun way for retirees to let their mind create wishes and then let their heads create strategies to turn those wishes into plans.

We want you to think about what your own retirement is going to look like. Many people assume their retirement will unfold like everyone else's. Too often, they are really clear on what they are retiring *from* but not entirely clear on what they are retiring *to*.

You have the opportunity to build the kind of life you want, and to accomplish some of the things you dreamt of when you thought you had all the time in the world. While we now know our time is not without limit, we have the experience that we can apply to make each of our moments count.'

Managing retirement stress

Retirement experts suggest the foundation of a good retirement rests on the retirees' ability to handle stress. There are a number of stressors in retirement that will challenge even the most successful retirees. Some of the stressors they may encounter are:

- Challenges to their health or that of their spouse.
- Changes in relationships with their family and friends.
- Emotional changes.
- A new home.
- Concern over financial uncertainty.
- Lack of structure or purpose.

Longevity studies tell us stress management is an important indicator of long-term retirement happiness. When we counsel retirees, we give them ways to strengthen their retirement personality. As an advisor, you can be sensitive to whether your client has a positive attitude towards this next phase and conduct your questioning with that in mind.

You could also put together a workshop on retirement opportunities, making sure to invite that client.

Let's look at some of the personal characteristics and practical steps people can take to have the best chance of a happy and satisfying retirement.

Four attributes of the ideal retirement personality

Control. Successful retirees feel they have control over the important parts of their lives. They tend to plan ahead for those predictable life events and are the first to find ways to put structure into their life in retirement. Even if they don't have control over such things as their health, they recognize they always have control over their attitude towards their health.

Commitment. Successful retirees are committed to living each and every day to the fullest. They know why they get out of bed in the morning and have an understanding of the basic values that govern their life.

Challenge. Successful retirees continue to challenge themselves to learn new things, to do new things and to create new life experiences. There is no genetic or psychological reason why we can't continue to challenge our minds as we get older. A 75-year-old woman who attended one of our workshops had recently completed her Executive MBA. There are many stories like this where retirees are furthering their education, developing new skills or pursuing new hobbies.

Connectedness. Successful retirees feel connected to their families, their community, their world and their spirituality. In other words, they understand their true life values and strive to live a life of purpose. Longevity studies tell us that this sense of purpose, from feeling part of a bigger picture, could actually add years to our lives.

At the foundation of this ideal retirement personality is an optimistic view on life. Did you know optimists live longer than pessimists?

Someone once said that happiness is not a destination but the way we live life each day. A happy person in retirement isn't happy just because they're retired. If your clients were miserable before retirement, retirement isn't likely to change their outlook on life.

One of the biggest challenges they will face in retirement will occur when they encounter one of those life-altering events that take their 'best laid plans' and turn them upside down. Life transitions are inevitable, but they're also stressful. If your client is an individual who has a hard time handling change in their life, they'll likely find their retirement a challenging time.

Here are some things you can encourage your clients to do to prepare themselves mentally for retirement:

- Set goals and plans to achieve in all areas of their life.
- Think of things they've always wanted to do and make plans to do them.
- Talk over their goals and plans with those who will share their retirement.
- Find experiences that will help them take risks
- Treat all problems as opportunities

Six practical steps to retirement success

The Retirement Lifestyle Center provides these six suggestions for retirees and prospective retirees:

Have a clear vision of the future. What is it you really want to do in this next phase of life? What would an ideal week in retirement actually look like? Many people think this phase will be one leisure activity after another. In fact, successful retirees create a structure for their retirement life that replaces the structure they had in the workplace.

Three questions communications expert Dan Sullivan poses to people might be particularly appropriate at this stage:

- If you won the lottery, would you change the way you spend your time?
- If you found out you only had five years to live, would that change how you live your life today?
- At your 80th birthday party, when your friends gather to honor you, what is it you would like them to say about you?

Practice good health and 'wellness'. Most retirees today can look forward to many years of happy retirement as long as they pay attention to the basic principles of healthy living. We think we'll see retirees paying more attention to how they can stay healthy as long as they can. Mental health is equally important in retirement as physical health. Retirees must find ways to stay mentally stimulated.

Maintain a positive view of 'work'. Retirement has always been defined as 'not working'. In fact, many retirees will generate some of their retirement income from a job. We are seeing many different approaches to work in retirement. Some people opt for gradual retirement, while others start their own business. Many retirees look at volunteering their time for causes they find fulfilling.

Rather than viewing retirement as freedom *from work*, it may be better for clients to view it as freedom *to work*.

Here are some strategies for change:

- Plan for another career 'after work'.
- Learn new skills.
- Talk to people who do what you dream of doing.
- Consider ways to stage retirement by job sharing or working part-time.
- Figure out your workplace strengths and skills, then look for opportunities to use them.
- Develop a 'second career' that you do while still working just for pure enjoyment.
- Maintain your workplace friendships beyond work.

Take a balanced approach to leisure. Leisure is the opportunity to do what you want, when you want. That's certainly one of the advantages of this next phase of life. However, retirees should look at balanced leisure rather than focus on just one or two activities. The 'paradox of leisure' is that we like leisure because it's a break from what we do – if you have leisure all the time, where's your break?

A balanced retirement should include the six basic types of leisure activity:

- Creative expression.
- Spectator appreciation.
- Physical activity.
- Solitary contemplation.
- Social interaction.
- Intellectual engagement.

Fulfil and support personal relationships. Retirement is a time to enjoy family and friends. In fact, these two groups contribute to many of the leisure activities that retirees find fulfilling. Retirement can be an isolating experience for some and retirees need to work on maintaining their social networks. We also find a lot of couples don't talk about their joint vision for their impending retirement. This is a time to make sure you're on the same page.

Find financial comfort. Financial comfort is different for all of us. Do you worry about money? Are you concerned you don't have enough? Do the ups and downs of the markets affect your outlook on retirement? Financial comfort may mean a client being able to spend what they want or it may mean having enough money to change their lifestyle. The key to financial comfort is having a plan for retirement and then a clear view of financial resources.

Find out more at www.retirementlifestyle.com.

Clarifying goals

So your client now has a picture of what they want retirement to look like and they are focused on the lifestyle they expect. But there's a big difference between a wish and reality. It's time to set some specific goals.

In turn, goals will remain daydreams unless your clients have a strategy in place to make them happen. Timelines and a set of clear actions motivate people to make progress.

Many people planning for their retirement make this a financial exercise when a broader life approach is required. For example, if a client intends to move home in retirement, they might start looking at real estate listings well beforehand and even try living in a location for a few weeks.

We feel it's important to have goals in nine different areas:

- Your work

- Your health

- Your financial situation

- Your family

- Your home

- Your community

- Your activities and hobbies

- Your personal development

- Your spirituality

In each area, your client needs to consider:

- What is it I need or want to do in each area?
- Why is this important?
- Why am I not doing it now?
- What are the specific steps I need to take?

In retirement planning, we take clients through a process of exploration and planning activities that lead them to actualizing their dream list.

We also try to help clients become comfortable with change, because in this fast-paced world, and as we age, things can change quickly. Your clients may be empty nesters now but an adult child could move back home while they study for a second university degree; your client may be healthy today but suffer a stroke tomorrow.

We suggest clients revisit their plans at least once every three years and be prepared to modify their dream list.

Developing a plan

A retirement plan covers a number of different areas of a client's life. The Life-First Advisor directs the client's focus to the important elements in their life plan rather than just the financial aspects.

Here are the major life areas and some financial considerations:

Financial implications

Life planning area	Some financial implications
Work	• Income replacement • Severance • Bonus • Phased-in retirement • Self-employment
Health	• Long-term care • Critical illness • Income replacement • Benefit programs
Money	• Adequate income • Return vs risk • Tax implications • Pension Plan contributions • Charitable giving • Healthy savings
Family	• Income protection • Health benefits • Education funding • Critical care for parents • Estate planning
Home	• Mortgage protection • Financing considerations • Renovations • Residence change • Vacation property • Investment property
Community	• Charitable giving • Team sponsorship
Leisure	• Vacation funding • Hobby costs • Budgeting • Income replacement
Mind	• Financial education • Goal setting for the future • Financial comfort
Spirit	• Legacy planning • Charitable giving or tithing • Estate planning • Travel budgeting

With so many clients on the verge of retirement, advisors are adding retirement lifestyle planning programs to their value-added service offering. Your clients are seeking information and they are getting it from many different places. What kind of information are you providing and how do you deliver it? Retirement planning is an opportunity to educate your clients about the things they may not be aware of, using your workshops, seminars, website and newsletters.

The Life-First Advisor ...

- Discovers how their client wants to live their life in retirement
- Helps them turn those wishes into specific goals
- Educates clients on the life issues that come with retirement, not just the financial ones

15 | Marketing to Older Clients

- **Marketing to older clients requires understanding their emotional hot buttons**

- **The 50-plus segment is not a homogenous group but concerns over safety, independence, health and meaning are often prominent**

- **The Life-first approach helps maturing clients understand important life issues they may not have thought about as they look at retirement**

More mature clients want an emotional attachment to their advisors, one based on a shared understanding of their needs.

Relationship marketing is not about a single event, such as a client appreciation day or a seminar, but a series of client contacts that reinforce the advisor's value proposition and create a positive emotional response.

In short, it's a process – one that focuses on building learning relationships. The financial planning aspects are packaged as solutions to needs identified by the maturing client in the learning process.

The goals of marketing to mature clients are to:

- Develop an emotional connection with the advisor.
- Focus on the benefits the advisor can provide.
- Develop client loyalty.
- Provide a tag the client can use to identify and remember the advisor.

Remember that marketing isn't just an exercise to bring in new clients. In fact, you're marketing each and every day to your current client base. Your ongoing marketing efforts are crucial to maintaining your relevance with your clients and continuing to be 'top of mind' when they need advice.

Marketing to the mature client isn't just about passing on information and hoping the listener will internalize the message, see its value and then make a decision to work with you.

Your marketing has to be targeted in a way that lets the recipient know you have something of value that will help them personally. You have to be a catalyst to enable the client to think about the important issues and then seek your help with the financial aspects.

A diverse market

The 50-plus market is a diverse one. Early retirees, for example, are still healthy, active, happy and interested in doing things. They've only just started tapping into their retirement savings and they haven't really felt the brunt of what it's like to live on a fixed income yet. Those closer to 70 and fully retired are likely to be far less willing to spend freely.

And, of course, varying life experiences, socio-economic status, ethnicity and personal characteristics mean older people hold a range of values, beliefs, and opinions as diverse as within the population in general. The world view of someone who grew up in the 1940s is bound to be different from someone raised in 1960s.

Tailoring messages for an older audience therefore means recognizing a multitude of differences about many issues:

- What constitutes 'the good life,' quality and service.
- Attitudes toward authority or bureaucracy.
- Degree of comfort in asking for help.
- Perceptions of health and illness.
- Attitudes toward disability.
- Ideas about food and nutrition.

- Concepts of age and aging.
- Gender roles.
- Family and intergenerational relationships.
- The role of government.
- Access to health and social services.

And while your service offering to younger clients may have been based on single-need solutions – such as investment funds or insurances policies – your offering to the 50-plus client will be based not on products but on life stage.

Emotional hot buttons

We know we become more emotion-centered, introspective and contextual as we age, so a key to effective communication with older clients and prospects is the ability to connect with their emotional 'hot buttons'.

Your solutions should focus on making them feel better about the things that cause them concern. Here are the six key emotional needs for a 50-plus client:

The need for safety. These clients tend to want to maintain the status quo, even though life conspires to make changes. Safety also speaks to their desire to avoid stress. Stress could come from worry over money, relationship problems, health concerns or personal security. When these stressors have a potential financial consequence, solutions should seek to protect them from unnecessary worry.

Protection from fear. Older people often fear unexpected events that could change the way they live their life or how they view the world. This also plays into the need for safety, in that your maturing clients want to ensure nothing catastrophic will affect their sense of security.

The need to be independent. The feeling of 'being in control' becomes important to your aging client. It represents a link to youth and personal empowerment. Your 50-plus client generally wants to feel they are 'still in charge' and not in a position where someone has to tell them what to do.

The need to belong. Maturing clients generally like to belong to groups or social organizations as a way of extending their social network. In addition, your 50-plus clients expect you to be aware of the issues associated with the biggest group they belong to – people over 50! That means your solutions, marketing approach and communications strategy should reflect your respect for their situation.

The importance of altruism. Altruism is an unselfish concern for others. This can become pronounced in a 50-plus client. Charitable giving, gifting loved ones, contributing to a grandchild's education or building a legacy are all examples of altruistic behavior. You would be well advised to include questions in your exploration process that draw out their need to be altruistic.

Search for meaning. The older we get the more contemplative or spiritual we can become. Studies suggest spirituality has a direct relationship to longevity. It's easier to get up in the morning if you feel life has purpose or meaning. Your role is to find ways to remind your client of who they are and where they are going. This is where the goal setting and strategy work comes in.

Becoming a 'life stage' marketer

The most effective approach to marketing to the mature market is to be a 'life stage' marketer. This is also called life-transition marketing and fits well with the Life-First Approach.

Like any aggregate consumer group, the 50-plus market is actually made up of a number of segments, with identifiable characteristics and hot buttons. Savvy marketers find it effective to divide this market into five age-related groups:

- Early Generation X and late Baby Boomers (ages 50-62 approximately).

- Early retirees (63-67).

- Fully retired (68-75).

- Later-stage retirement (75-89).

- Elders (80+).

Let's look at some of the common emotional issues and financial concerns within each segment.

Concerns by segment

Life Phase	Common emotional issues	Common financial concerns
Early Gen X/Late Boomers	<ul><li>Work uncertainty</li><li>Contemplating retirement</li><li>Empty nesting</li><li>Helping children get established</li><li>Awareness of mortality</li><li>Health challenges</li><li>Care of parents</li></ul>	<ul><li>Income replacement</li><li>Retirement readiness</li><li>Tax efficiency</li><li>Pension plan options</li><li>Real estate purchase or sale</li><li>Reassessing insurance</li><li>Benevolence</li><li>Financing post-secondary education</li><li>Savings maximization</li><li>Change in risk profile or asset allocation</li><li>Estate settlement (parents)</li></ul>
Early Retirees	<ul><li>Health concerns (personal, spouse)</li><li>Adjustment to retirement</li><li>Change in social network</li><li>Self-improvement</li><li>Leisure opportunities</li><li>Benevolence</li></ul>	<ul><li>Income conversion</li><li>Household budgeting</li><li>Pension plan benefits or conversion</li><li>Real estate purchase or sale</li><li>Change in risk profile or asset allocation</li><li>Long-term care concerns (self and parents)</li><li>Insurance conversion</li><li>Financial assistance to children or grandchildren</li><li>Estate settlement</li></ul>
Fully Retired	<ul><li>Bereavement (friends, family)</li><li>Health limitations</li><li>Decline in social network</li><li>Change in leisure opportunities</li><li>Change in residence</li><li>Benevolence</li></ul>	<ul><li>Retirement savings plan conversion</li><li>Estate settlement</li><li>Change in risk profile or asset allocation</li><li>Estate planning</li><li>Change in spending pattern</li><li>Gifting or planned giving</li><li>Managing finances on own</li></ul>
Late-stage retirement / Elders	<ul><li>End of life issues</li><li>Bereavement</li><li>Health limitations</li><li>Benevolence</li><li>Helping family</li><li>Change in residence</li><li>Long-term or chronic care</li></ul>	<ul><li>Estate considerations</li><li>Change in spending pattern</li><li>Gifting or planned giving</li><li>Sharing financial management</li></ul>

Core values of the older client

Older clients have core values they've lived by all their lives. When they buy something it has to fit one or more of these values.

A recent survey found that older people put most value on self-respect, family ties and religion. These were followed closely by warm relationships, compassion, intellectual curiosity, health, happiness, conservatism and financial security. These respondents valued materialism, excitement and social power the least.

Of course, that's one survey and the values of your older clients will vary widely, depending on their backgrounds, cultural differences and personal choices. The important thing is to become familiar with your clients' and prospects' attitudes, values and beliefs and let that inform your marketing efforts.

Here are some categories a group of US sociologists has used to describe different sets of values and beliefs:

True Blue Believers are religious but not zealous, happy but not giddy, smart but not brilliant, conservative but not inflexible. Older people in this category have found their 'place' in life. They are fulfilled and happy in their circle of family and friends. They can afford to be modest in their lives. They do not feel they have anything to prove.

Hearth & Homemakers have family and friends at the center of their lives, and their church is the center of their community. The hospital receptionist knows them personally as frequent visitors and volunteers. Their memories are rich and full and they see their life as happy and rewarding.

Fiscal Conservatives have achieved the good life and are admired for their possessions and accomplishments. They are careful shoppers who buy quality over value. They are keen on tradition and family pride and wary of change for themselves, their family and their community.

Intense Individualists see the world as tough and unforgiving and have a sense of resourcefulness and self-reliance. They can be unsentimental and uncompromising and assume a clear leadership role with their family and community.

Active Achievers have decided not to be 'old'. They expect to be successful as they age. People in this category are well educated, socially involved and prosperous. They are non-conformists who thrive on excitement. The active achievers are more likely to be divorced and will place less emphasis on close family ties.

Liberal Loners have a strong sense of purpose and desire for independence from government, financial restraints, health-care institutions, friends and family. They value honesty and social equality. Even though they have a social conscience, they do not always have the energy to translate empathy into action.

In-Charge Intellectuals are the elite of society. They are life-long readers and thinkers who keep up with social change. They are secure in their ability and perception of the world. Their personal relationships are practical and casual. They are 'complete' and have few expectations of others.

Woeful Worriers have some memory of much tougher times, which means financial security is a major priority. They are concerned about their health, home, companionship and social activities. They turn to religion for support and believe the meaning of faith is following the rules and honoring the beliefs they were brought up with.

The benefit of diversity

Given this diversity, financial advisors have a tremendous opportunity to use their knowledge and particular approach as a point of difference in the market.

In many professions – accountancy for example – people specialize in servicing particular demographic groups. In the financial services industry, however, most advisors base their marketing on helping clients of every age manage their money. In other words, they market what they do rather than their ability to help those they do it for.

Advisors who specialize in retirement planning will also have clients of all ages who will benefit from their expertise. However, the main focus of their practice is that they are a 50-plus specialist. Their marketing efforts are geared towards letting professional referral sources, other advisors, personal coaches and their present and potential clients know they specialize in issues relating to this age group.

You can choose to specialize in the issues that will affect an aging population, and differentiate and brand yourself because you have done so. There are two parts to this specialization:

- The 'science' of being a 50-plus advisor, which means understanding the key issues that your clients will face and being able to access other professionals in your community who can help.

- The 'art' of being a 50-plus advisor, which addresses how you market the work you have done in providing services to the mature marketplace.

It's important to increase your knowledge of those life areas that are going to impact on the thinking of those in your market. It's equally important for you to be seen to be doing so!

Seven Deadly Sins

Your clients are maturing (we don't like to say 'getting older') and the way you relate to them through your communications and marketing strategies has to speak to the psychological and physiological changes arising from the aging process.

However, many advisors miss opportunities to connect with maturing clients because they fail to recognize basic challenges their clients face. Here are the seven most common mistakes when dealing with 50-plus clients:

Treating a 50-plus client in the same way you treat a 35-year-old. The way you talk to a client, the services you market to them and the nature of your discussions with them all change as the client ages. If you fail to keep your messaging up to date, you risk sending conflicting signals and finding you become less and less relevant to older age groups.

Not understanding the context within which a retiring client views his or her life. A maturing client is much more likely to think in terms of "it's not money that's important but what money does!" For the advisor, that means recognizing where a senior client is in life and understanding how they see the world. Context can be as simple as 'connecting the dots' for the senior client, relating everything you say back to what it means to them in terms of their life.

Not appreciating the non-financial issues that will affect the way a client views money. As people age, issues such as health, relationships, bereavement, caregiving and empty nesting often crowd out purely financial concerns. Money issues ultimately will be driven by these non-financial concerns and the senior advisor has to understand how the two relate. Given the greater prominence of the right brain as we age, a 'smart' advisor is regarded as less valuable than a 'caring' advisor.

Not building intergenerational or inter-gender relationships. As clients age, they become more focused on family issues. Whether their concern is helping children or grandchildren, helping parents or worrying about a spouse, your client will be often preoccupied or driven by family. That will affect their financial planning decisions and the screen they use to process your information. Failure to consider their feelings about family may lead to an ineffective conversation that simply doesn't resonate with them. In later life, wealth transfer between spouses or to children becomes of greater concern. Advisors must cultivate positive relationships with spouses, parents and children.

Over-generalizing and not treating mature clients as individuals. Not all Boomers are the same and the advisor has to recognize that communicating and marketing to them as if they were one generation will likely fail to resonate with many. The older clients get, the more they wish to relate to a person and the more important a personal relationship becomes. For the advisor, that means tailoring all information specifically to the needs of the older client. The concept of 'one size fits all' doesn't work well with a mature client who wants an advisor who understands them personally. Successful advisors in the senior market spend more time getting to know their clients, including such things as family relationships, attitudes towards life issues and hopes and fears about the future.

Treating retirement as a financial or workplace issue. Retirement is as much a psychological issue as it is a leisure state. Retirement doesn't mean the same thing to each client and it's not always a happy picture or driven by achieving financial goals. For the client who isn't yet retired, there's often a tremendous sense of uncertainty about the future. For those who have just left work behind there can be feelings of inadequacy or uselessness. Successful advisors will spend more time helping the client recognize the issues. In fact, the most powerful phrase might be, "Have you thought about ... ?"

Not paying attention to the special needs of mature women. Our experience in all of the countries where we work has been that the typical advisor-client relationship is a male advisor working with a male client. However, demographics tell us the chances of the woman becoming the sole decision maker at some point are above 90 percent. In short, the inter-gender transfer of wealth will become as big an issue for advisors as the intergenerational transfer of wealth. Women have different issues and concerns than most men. Concerns about family, caregiving, household budgeting, health and planning for longevity change the way many women look at money and advice.

Successful boomer advisors set themselves apart because of their focus on the client rather than on investment or financial planning. That means gaining an overall understanding of all the important issues that will be on the minds of their aging clients.

The Life-First Advisor ...

- Shows sensitivity to the particular concerns and issues of older clients
- Builds an emotional connection with the client
- Acknowledges the diversity of values among older groups
- Understands issues around intergenerational and inter-gender wealth transfer

16 | Communicating with Older Clients

- **Communications should be adjusted for older clients**
- **Older clients tend to more right-brain focused and less mentally flexible**
- **Their less acute vision and hearing also must be considered**
- **Building trust goes a long way to overcoming these obstacles**

Senior citizens, 'golden oldies' ... these are euphemisms your older clients don't appreciate, along with other reminders of their age. The fact is, what we used to think of as 'old age' is changing.

Populations are rapidly ageing in many developed economies. People are living longer and spending three decades or more in retirement. Higher standards of living and health care mean people are much more active in what was formerly thought of as years of rest and decline.

In marketing to older people, advisors must do more than talk their language, they must make it easy for them to read and respond to that marketing.

The 50-plus audience doesn't necessarily like to multitask and reacts negatively to clutter. They respond positively to simplicity and clearly stated savings opportunities. They also prefer sound bites to diatribes.

A marketing strategy focused on the older market, combined with relationship selling, active networking and collaborating on goals will provide advisors with many opportunities for growth and profit.

Many experts believe relationship selling and marketing is a process that should never stop. This is even truer with older clients. They want to buy and they want the service that a relationship provides.

Different perspectives

	35-year-old	65-year-old	Relevance
World view	▪ Black and white	▪ Shades of grey	▪ Experience means older clients are wary of 'absolutes'. A blanket statement accepted by younger market may be met by 'prove it'.
Drawing inferences	▪ More likely to draw inferences	▪ Less likely to 'connect the dots'	▪ Older client must want to be 'engaged' first, then they'll give you their time and think about what you're saying
Context	▪ Less in need of context	▪ More in need of context	▪ Older clients need to understand how things affect them. 'Tell me what this means and why I should care.'
Mental flexibility	▪ More likely to change their mind	▪ Less likely to change their mind	▪ The older we get, the more our beliefs are fixed. 'Anything requiring a change in my belief system had better be effective'
Emotional bias	▪ More left-brain	▪ More right-brain	▪ The older the client the more right-brain or emotion-based the decision-making – regardless of gender
Multi-tasking	▪ More likely to multi-task	▪ Less likely to multi-task	▪ While older clients know they can multi-task, why should they bother?
Speed of processing	▪ Generally quicker	▪ Generally slower	▪ It's not that older clients can't think quickly – it's that they recognize good decisions should be well thought through.

Communication issues

The natural process of aging affects all five of the senses over time. The effect of aging on our eyesight and hearing are particularly important when it comes to communications.

Often, these sensory changes are gradual. You may not notice an older client is experiencing hearing problems or that they can't see as well as they used to. In fact, they may not recognize or admit to the changes themselves.

Eyesight

Several conditions can affect an older person's ability to read material, see an advertisement or even engage in a face-to-face conversation. Diseases such as age-related macular degeneration, glaucoma or cataracts can affect a person's ability to receive and process new information.

As we age, our lenses yellow and our ability to distinguish contrasts decreases. These conditions are also magnified by the lack of light or by glare.

Presbyopia is the culprit when it comes to reading something that is close to you. Most start to experience this around age 40 and by 50 you typically need a good pair of reading glasses within easy reach. In fact, 100 percent of the adult population in their 50s is affected by the condition to some degree. [20]

From a physiological standpoint, it may seem as if your arms are too short to read what's in front of you but it's really a decline in the elasticity in the lens of your eyes. A younger person's eyes are more able to make adjustments to accommodate looking at something close up than those of an older person.

For that reason, advisors need to make adjustments in their communication, using bigger fonts on business cards and other material.

---

[20] Kitchen, Clive, *Fact and Fiction of Health Vision: Eye care for adults and children*, 2007

With colors, older people can find it hard to distinguish contrasts where blue is used. The aging process often restricts the amount of light that reaches our photoreceptors, making bright yellow look brown and darker blues look black.

Advertisers compensate by using large text and bright colors, while ensuring there's lots of contrast between them to make it easier for seniors to see.

Another suggestion is to avoid stylistic fonts with inconsistent stroke widths. This is because the aging eye requires typefaces that function well under low-vision conditions. In general, sans serif fonts such as Arial or Helvetica work well.

Other good ideas are to:

- Use a minimum 12pt font in written material and 8pt on business cards.
- Avoid glossy paper for written materials.
- Watch color contrasts – the blue end of the spectrum is the danger zone. The best color contrast is basic black on white (not white on black).
- Use bright colors wherever possible.
- However, take care with reds and yellows, which can connote the need for caution.

Hearing

As with eyesight, hearing loss tends to be gradual. The process begins on average in the early 50s. After 65, more than half of people have some form of hearing loss.[21]

For those advisors whose communication is primarily the spoken word, hearing loss among clients presents an additional challenge. Many people will deny there's a problem and use coping mechanisms

---

[21] Fuller, Nona, "Unidentified Hearing Loss", quoted by The Hearing Institute of the US, 2005

such as lip reading or asking speakers to repeat what they said or speak more loudly. Worse, they may pretend they hear what you said.

There's a direct correlation between hearing loss and depression in seniors. People can feel hopeless, disinclined to start relationships or even talk to others because of poor hearing.[22]

Presbycusis is the term for gradual hearing loss due to aging. Some of the most common symptoms are:

- Others' speech sounds mumbled or slurred.
- High-pitched sounds such as 's' and 'th' are more difficult to hear and tell apart.
- Conversations are more difficult to understand, particularly when there's background noise.
- A man's voice is easier to hear than a higher-pitched woman's voice.
- Certain sounds seem overly loud.
- In some cases, people suffer from tinnitus (ringing in the ears).[23]

High-tone deafness is common after the mid-50s. Listeners have trouble hearing tones in the higher frequencies. That means it's counter-productive to raise your voice with these people in an effort to be heard. You are more likely to be heard if you lower the pitch of your voice.

Here are some tips for communicating with seniors whose hearing is impaired:

- Maintain a distance of three to six feet (1 to 2 metres).
- Face the person. Hard-of-hearing seniors tend to read lips.
- Don't yell or speak loudly. Talk slowly and in a low voice.
- Enunciate.
- Eliminate extra noise such as music or TV.
- Be prepared to restate what you said (not just repeat).
- Ask the client to repeat the information back to you, to be sure they got it.

---

[22] "Hearing loss in adults", Hearing Foundation of the US, 2007
[23] National Institute on Deafness and Other Communication Disorders, 2002

The telephone is one of the least effective means of communicating with older people. It's not only impersonal but potentially also an impediment if the client is hard of hearing. If the older person doesn't acknowledge hearing impairment, the person on the other end has no way of knowing whether the message is getting across. At least with a face-to-face conversation you can 'read' body signals to see if you are being heard.

Sensory change

Sensory change	Types of communication affected
Visual acuity	Product labeling, signage, street signs, brochures and other written communication, computer screens, televised information, glossy publications
Hearing acuity	Interpersonal communications, public address systems, telephone contact, television and radio, seminars and meetings
Agility and mobility	Push button telephones, banking machines, kits (to be assembled), packaging, opportunities to see billboards, ads etc.

Brain changes

Cognitive psychologists have established that as the brain ages, certain types of cognitive capacities change.

Processing speed. Older adults take longer to recall information and complete tasks. This affects their ability to carry out tasks that require visual perception, such as locating figures in a chart.

Cognitive flexibility. They're are less able to change their judgments when they're given additional information. They tend to make decisions based on their intuition, experience, and first impression – and then stick with it.

Capacity to draw inferences from information. The older the individual, the more difficult it is to read between the lines and to come to a conclusion based on the information.
Capacity to manipulate several types of information simultaneously. They have more difficulty multi-tasking. It's difficult for them to recall multiple details, such as a phone number, a person's name or the significance of that person, and why they need to return a call.

Ability to focus. As people age, they find it harder to eliminate distractions and focus on specific information. Some researchers believe this inability to rule out irrelevant details clutters the working memory, making it difficult to handle several types of information simultaneously and process new information.

These all represent psychological, neural and social reasons why the older audience may differ from the younger client. When you consider the physiological barriers we discussed earlier, the challenge becomes even greater.

Getting them to listen

One of the biggest challenges that communicators have in reaching older adults is in framing a message that will resonate with this audience.

They say that "with age comes experience". Unfortunately, it can also come with some set ideas about the world and less willingness to learning new things.

The challenge of communicating with older clients extends beyond finding reasoned arguments or devising something catchy that will spark their attention. The greater challenge is getting them to listen to the message in the first place.

This is why establishing trust is so important. When we trust someone we are more likely to listen to them, because we believe they have our best interests at heart. We also tend to listen if we like the communicator (the principle of rapport) or we respect their position or knowledge (the principle of authority).

While there's no guarantee people will automatically listen or internalize a message even from someone they trust, they are more likely to pay attention out of respect. We learn from our trust relationships and are less likely to 'tune them out'.

Bit by bit, older brains become more "right-brain dominant", which means it's easier to process inputs presented as sensory or emotional images, rather than data-driven, abstract, informational content.

So, having established trust, one of the most powerful ways to tap into the right brain is story-telling. Look back at Chapter 2 to remind yourself of this connection. With older clients now more right-brain focused, it's an important tool for this group.

The Life-First Advisor ...

- Tailors information to older clients that recognizes their perspective
- Makes allowances for visual and hearing impairment in their communication strategy
- Uses stories to communicate concepts through the right brain

17 | Behavioral Finance

- **Risk is a right-brain concept – it's an emotional topic**
- **When clients have an emotional reaction, pure logic is not necessarily the best response**
- **Understanding behavioral biases will help you build stronger, deeper relationships with clients**

Janetis a financial advisor based on the Gold Coast in Australia who prides herself on her comprehensive approach to financial planning. "I try to look at the whole picture and build plans for my clients that consider all the aspects of their life", she says.

Recently, though, she found herself having to spend more time talking to clients about investment performance – reminding them of the way markets move and reassuring them their plan is built to withstand difficult times.

"We've never spent a lot of time on investment performance discussions", she says, "but now I'm in the position of having to defend equity investments in general and the quality of my past advice".

Market volatility has always been with us, but over the past decade we've seen some pretty radical moves in investment markets. The speed of transactions, global access to information and computerized trading are among the things that have conspired to give investors a whole new experience, along with uncertain economic conditions.

At times, the fear of losing their retirement nest eggs has been palpable for many, and some normally rational, mature people have contemplated cashing out and heading for the exit.

This presents a tremendous challenge for investment and financial advisors who made sound recommendations but are being questioned by their clients at such times. What do you say to a client who is so afraid of the future you can't get through to them with logic and reason?

Risk is a right-brain concept

The most common way advisors help clients understand market volatility is to show them charts of past performance and to remind them that investing is a long-term proposition. "It's a marathon, not a sprint" and "It's time in the market that matters, not timing the market" are two adages used to help clients understand how to invest in equities.

Advisors and product providers may use advertising to focus clients on the fact that "we've seen this before" or "the markets go on sale every time they fall". To support these statements they trot out every chart they can find that illustrates the positive long-term trend in equity markets.

They're right: over the long run it's better to participate in the long-term growth of quality businesses. Why, then, won't clients listen to reason? Why do they panic whenever they see a sudden reversal in market fortunes? How is an advisor supposed to address risk and volatility in a way that will make clients feel better about the financial plans they've made?

The discussion of risk isn't actually about market performance or the logic of investing for the long term. If it were, advisors would have no difficulty explaining market volatility and getting clients to dollar-cost average whenever markets fall.

When clients are concerned about losing their money, they're not usually pacified or enlightened by charts, facts and past performance. They have a real fear their life will change in some way because of a reversal in investment markets. In some cases, they regret making the original decision to invest in the first place. They may also be thinking that 'whatever can go wrong will go wrong!'

Some investors even make market reversals personal. Consider the client who tells you, "If I buy it, it will probably go down". Such sentiments have nothing to do with logic but everything to do with emotion. They're right-brain issues, not left-brain opinions based on sound reasoning.

Ultimately, you're unlikely to counter emotion with logic, which is why the approach most advisors take with worried investors misses the mark.

To understand how clients view risk, let's look closely at some behavioral finance concepts.

Behavioral finance and risk

At the level of the individual investor, behavioral finance could be considered the study of why smart people do dumb things. It's used to explain the difference between rational and irrational behavior. By applying psychology to economic and market theory, it seeks to explain the difference between the 'ideal' and the 'reality'.

In behavioral finance, the rational investor is called *homo economicus*. This mythical individual always acts with perfect self-interest and invests in an environment where all knowledge is available on which to make informed decisions.

In a perfect world, your clients would understand that market ebbs and flows are normal and that things usually work out in the long run if they just hang in there.

Unfortunately, that's not how most investors view life. They often use their own 'rules of thumb' – which scientists call 'heuristics' – to guide investment decisions. Clients have created a basic structure that determines how they view the world and it has become part of their crystallized thinking (see Chapter 2).

This internal rationale will override many of your best arguments.

When you try to explain risk by using numbers, past performance or logic you're appealing to the common sense of the rational investor. There's nothing wrong with this approach if you're actually dealing with an investor who will see the same things you do.

However, if your client blocks out your explanations with their own 'self talk' or because of their own view of the world, all your sound reasoning is wasted.

We recently listened to a talk by one of North America's most respected advisor 'gurus', who said that if clients didn't listen to your explanation about the long-term performance of markets you should 'fire them' and move on. The idea was that there are lots of potential clients who *will* listen to your historical perspective.

But this commentator is confusing the fact that the client won't listen to reason with the client being 'obtuse'. We're not convinced. Just because a client doesn't buy into your unassailable logic about how markets work doesn't mean you can't help them.

Behavioral biases

Behavioral biases change the client's perspective on rational ideas.

You may have thought you and your client agreed on an investment strategy – a passive investment strategy, for example, that focuses on the client's goals rather than on where the markets are. But now the markets have fallen and the client is listening to some investment 'genius' on TV. All bets are off as your client reacts to short-term moves in the market and completely forgets what you talked about.

If you leave your client alone and don't try to counter their biases you run the risk they'll continue to question your advice and re-evaluate or discard their plans.

But rather than throwing history and logic at them, a better approach is to try to understand their reaction and the effect short-term movements are having on their view of 'risk'. By understanding what's behind your client's fears you can develop a strategy to mitigate or counter them.

Biases can be either cognitive (where the client recognizes the bias but often acts on faulty information) or emotional (where they react subconsciously). To make your job even tougher, emotional and cognitive biases usually work against each other, with emotional biases winning the day.

This often results in overreaction, or unwarranted optimism or pessimism. In the case of the client who is starting to panic about markets, pessimism can become manic – the client envisions all sorts of ways things could go wrong. Remember, this isn't as much about understanding markets as it is about emotional paralysis.

If you want to talk to your client about risk, the nature of the bias will determine your approach. Let's examine the most common biases that affect the client's view of risk and how you might address them.

Cognitive dissonance

When your client receives information that appears to conflict with what they thought they knew, this creates cognitive dissonance or a mental 'imbalance'.

Let's say you've talked to your client about how you take a long-term view of markets and that the short term doesn't matter. One day the market takes a big hit, and your client forgets everything you talked about. They're now torn between what they thought they knew versus what they see and hear in the media. You're no longer the trusted advisor – someone like Cramer on CNBC or Kochie on Channel 7 in Australia is.

That can create cognitive dissonance and result in a client 'starting all over again' when it comes to understanding markets.

The best way to mitigate cognitive dissonance is to continue to hammer home your message, reminding your client of the goals and strategies you set together.

This messaging has to have been done from the start of the relationship – and every time you talk – to have maximum effect.

Think of it this way: if someone came along and put a handprint on your painting you'd either have to touch up the mistake or start all over again. Of course, if the paint had already 'set' a hand on it wouldn't matter. When you educate your client, or create a common understanding, you have to make sure the paint 'sets' so the idea is firmly entrenched in their mind. The more entrenched, the harder it will be for another idea to replace it.

You reinforce learning if you constantly manage your client's expectations. By discussing both the positive and negative potential of an investment you help the client recognize 'normal' market behavior when it occurs.

Too many advisors are afraid to address the potential negatives when they develop a strategy. That will come back to bite them when things inevitably take a turn south.

If your client is questioning your advice in the face of conflicting information, your main task is to re-establish trust by sitting down with them to review the original plan.

Self-attribution

Have you ever noticed that when an idea works out clients think it was their idea, but if it fails it's yours?

Self-attribution is a cognitive bias that's often tied up with ego. The client wants to be a willing participant in the planning process but views positive information on an investment as a personal triumph. If the news is good we're talking about *my* money. If the news is bad we're talking about *your* advice.

When markets disappoint, it's natural for clients to question the advice they've been given. It's no longer the markets they distrust but the advisor. That makes them more open to 'a second opinion' and they may move their money to the next 'guru' if they find advice they like.

In fact, some researchers theorize that investors will hire an advisor simply because they're looking for a scapegoat. William O'Barr and John Conley suggest in their book *Fortune and Folly: The Wealth and Power of Institutional Investing* that this is quite common.

There will also be clients who move their money out of the market but want to continue their relationship with you. In that case, they trust you – just not your investment advice.

Advisors who find themselves in this position must be as open as possible about why they made the recommendation in the first place. If they still believe in the viability of the original investment they have to remind the client about the benefits regardless of market action.

This should lead to the dollar-cost-averaging discussion, where the client may be more open to the idea that the investment just 'went on sale'.

Ambiguity aversion

People avoid taking risks if they're uncertain about the future or not sure they're doing the right thing.

If your client is influenced by ambiguity aversion their fear may have nothing to do with markets or the investment strategy you suggest. Instead, they might be feeling overwhelmed by their overall view of the world or the outlook for markets and the economy.

Advisor: *George and Mary, it would be my advice that we develop a plan to provide for some future growth to protect you from inflation and to give you a more balanced approach to your investment strategy.*

Client: *We'll think about it, but with so much going on around the world and with stock markets being so scary I think we'll just wait until things calm down a bit.*

It's common for clients to get caught up in bad news that may surround the markets or economy. In fact, it's unavoidable. What's more, you may be contributing to your client's sense that short-term noise is important each time you send out a market commentary intended to keep them informed.

An advisor we know sends out a market update each Friday. He obviously spends a lot of time researching and composing it each week and it can stretch to several pages covering the performance and outlook of investment classes, as well as economic news. Asked why he does this, he said his clients expected it and he liked to keep them up to date.

An unintended effect of his weekly updates, however, is that he's making the short term more important than it need be. He's unwittingly conditioning clients to see his advice in a short-term light. They may now feel they should examine their own investments every week.

Loss aversion

We have a natural tendency to fear loss. This fear is present in most people even when they seem like they're buying in to what you're saying.

Did you know that, as a motivator, the possibility of a loss is, on average, twice as powerful as the possibility of making a gain of the same magnitude? This anomaly is known as 'prospect theory' and suggests investors are actually more willing to take risks to avoid a loss than they are to take risks to make a gain. Daniel Kahneman won a Nobel Prize in Economics for his work on this.

Behavioral finance expert Meir Statman formulated his 'fear of regret' theory to explain why investors engage in risky behavior simply to avoid loss. Statman says investors often let ego get in the way and are unwilling to admit they may have made a 'bad' investment.

While you can't guarantee your client will never experience a loss, you should help them understand that they could crystalize losses if they move away from the plan they accepted and had you execute for them – for example, if they panic and sell in the midst of a downturn for fear their holdings are heading to zero.

Often, the fear of loss actually has more to do with the impact of volatility on an investment than the possibility the client could lose his or her money by holding on. Theoretically, if the client equates risk with volatility then they also equate taking away volatility with eliminating risk.

Some clients may understand that immediately, and then you can have a discussion about how holding an asset for a long time decreases volatility, hence decreasing the risk.

However, not all clients will be so easily pacified. The more fearful among them may be losing sleep worrying about the future – logic and dollar-cost-averaging concepts are not likely to succeed with them.

In this case, appeal to a client's emotional center by showing them you're not worried and that you'll work with them to manage the ups and downs in the market.

Don't make the discussion about the markets, and do not become an apologist for how the markets perform. Your role is to act as the client's coach and partner through all kinds of market conditions.

Here's some language you could use:

George, when we created our strategy, we did so with the understanding there would always be 'ups and downs' that might occur at any time. It's my job to identify the best investment strategies to help you reach the goals you set. I want to reassure you I'm continuing to monitor the ability of the strategies and investments we advised, and you agreed upon, to fit your plan and give you a positive experience and a reasonable chance to help you achieve all that's important to you. If ever I feel there are better alternatives, my role is to provide you that advice at the time, and your role is to weigh that advice and consider making a change.

Conservatism

The older clients get, the more conservative they are likely to become. This bias is considered cognitive but also has emotional elements.

As clients look at their nest egg, they factor in the time it would take to recoup any losses that might be incurred as markets move around. Common sense suggests a 60-year-old would look at the possibility of loss in a much different way than a 30-year-old.

As your client moves towards retirement, there's a tendency to focus on the aging process and the desire to maintain the status quo. This need for stability is called 'continuity theory' and refers to how people become more resistant to change with age. Consider it a coping mechanism to help make sense of getting older.

The possibility of an investment loss might shake the foundations of the client's life and lead to more change than the client is willing to take on.

Consider this scenario: The client bases future goals, income needs and lifestyle on known financial resources. This provides a sense of financial comfort that comes from knowing where they stand. But over the course of half a year, that nest egg has shrunk by 10 percent. The client struggles to cope with a change in future expectations based on a smaller nest egg but also with the fear that the nest egg will shrink even further.

Now emotion takes over, leading to further irrational thoughts. 'What if I have to return to work? What if I have to keep working for a long time? What if I am forced to change my lifestyle?'

Suddenly, the client starts to exhibit 'emotional intransigence'. Their future is at stake and you're trying to tell them 'this is just a blip' or that 'markets will inevitably recover'.

One mistake advisors make at this point is to talk to a client about investment time horizon. While it's logical that a 60-year-old client might still have 25 or 30 years ahead of them, that doesn't always make emotional sense to the client.

As people age, they become much more introspective and aware of their mortality. As a result, the concept of investment time horizon moves from chronological to psychological.

From the client's perspective, they could live 30 years or 30 days and they're not willing to bet on either one! Now you're telling them they could live through many more market cycles. And you can't figure out why they don't listen to reason?

The best way to approach the conservatism bias is to recognize another behavioral bias known as 'mental accounting'. This refers to the tendency clients have to segment various financial assets and to treat each one in a different way psychologically.

Mental accounting and framing

The negative side to mental accounting is that it can cause a client to ignore the big picture, focusing them in on one element of their investment portfolio. A well-crafted asset allocation strategy can be undone because the client becomes concerned about the performance of just one of its components.

However, you can use mental accounting to your advantage when dealing with a conservative client who's afraid of investment loss. Consider this exchange between a prospect and advisor:

Prospect: *I don't know what I'm going to do now that I've lost 30 percent of my retirement portfolio in the past year. Can you help me recoup my losses?*

Advisor: *Just so I'm clear, which part of your retirement portfolio did you lose?*

This reply would no doubt elicit a quizzical look from the prospect.

Prospect: *What do you mean, 'which part of my retirement portfolio'? My retirement portfolio doesn't have parts.*

Actually, it does if the original advisor set it up with the client properly. If you're managing the nest egg of a conservative client, particularly when it comes to retirement money, you should help the client understand the various segments of the portfolio.

There's a way to segment a retirement portfolio for a client to help them understand how each component has a different investment strategy. Have them think of their overall portfolio in terms of what each component part is supposed to do. This can be accomplished in your discovery process by asking the client what kinds of assets they have that would fill these three 'banks':

The Essentials bank pays for food, clothing and shelter and provides for all the expenses considered essential to the lifestyle of the client. The money that goes in this bank consists of pensions, guaranteed investment payments, government benefits and systematic withdrawals from a portfolio.

The Lifestyle bank is for regular but discretionary spending, as well as lifestyle expenditure the client would like to make in the coming year. This pays for those things that make life enjoyable – things like travel, entertainment and gifts.

The Nest Egg bank contains the resources that allow a client to sleep at night, that reassure them they're 'going to be OK'. This bank includes things like long-term pensions and savings, inheritances, real estate and business assets.

By using mental accounting to help the client understand that each bank has a different role in their overall plan, fear can be attached to one of the banks without the client worrying about all three.

Framing is the concept of presenting information in a way that makes it easier for a client to take a fresh look at strategy and move away from limiting biases. In the case of the three banks, the advisor is able to change the client's idea that there's just one portfolio and it's all at risk.

Since each bank could be invested in a different manner, the client would be less likely to panic over market losses. They need no longer fear their lifestyle is at risk.

It's a simple approach, to be sure. But we've seen it work with affluent clients simply by getting them to reorganize their thinking as they look at their investment portfolio.

Ultimately, they do spend money out of their investment portfolio and current income to fund all three life areas. But mental accounting allows them to consider the role played by each of the component parts of a portfolio. That takes some of the fear away.

Framing is a terrific strategy. If you can move the discussion away from a comparison of where the client is in relation to the markets to where the client is in relation to their goals, you're no longer focusing on short-term market risk.

Helping clients understand risk biases

We assess our client's risk tolerance and we assume they understand their own risk tolerance too. But we've all seen fear of risk rear its head at the slightest provocation. Here are some ways to incorporate your understanding of behavioral finance into the work you do with clients, to help them cope with market moves when they occur:

'A stitch in time saves nine'. Your initial discussions with clients must address the various aspects of risk that can present over the life of an investment. Don't scare the client, but establish what is 'normal' market behavior.

Don't be an apologist or cheerleader for the markets. You use equities as part of a thought-out strategy to give your client the most positive investment experience over the life of their plan. Avoid trying to 'justify' the ebbs and flows of markets. Limit your discussions of markets to those of a spectator rather than in your role as an advisor.

Limit your market communication or commentary. If you suggest via your communications that the short term is important, how can you expect clients not to react to it? If you must have market commentary, make it a 'drop-down' on your website and limit it to a quick summary in your newsletter.

Let clients know risk management is integral to what you do. You are your client's primary advisor in picking the right managers to manage their nest egg. Your risk management strategy is to use diversification and asset allocation to mitigate overall risk. These strategies were put in place to manage through short-term fluctuations and protect their long-term goals.

Ensure they know you are more concerned about where *they* are than where the markets are. Reinforce the role you play in the life of your client as their primary advisor, not investment advisor. Emphasize that your expertise is in understanding the client and where they are in their life, rather than predicting short-term moves by markets.

The 'right' questions

The discussion about risk lends itself to a conversation with your client, more than a presentation. After all, you're trying to understand your client before you try to get them to understand you.

Your client's fears and concerns may not be rational, but they're real. Helping them think through the issues is the best strategy.

Here are some the questions you should ask to help you and your client confront the fear issue:

- Can you help me understand what concerns you the most about this investment/market/economy ... ?

- What do you think is making you feel this way?

- If this scenario occurred, how would it affect your life today and the assets you already have?

- What's the worst thing you can see happening if you implement this strategy?

- What might be some of the implications for your long-term plan if you don't implement this strategy, or make changes to it now?

Understanding behavioral finance means you'll be able to help investors make better decisions, with clients who understand behavioral finance able to handle market volatility better. Knowledge of investor psychology will deepen your relationships with clients.

Addressing behavioral bias

Behavioral bias	Client behavior	Strategies to talk about 'risk'
Cognitive Dissonance *A conflict between what they have been taught and what they experience today*	▪ Client seems to forget original discussion or the benefits of the plan that is in place. ▪ Client is questioning validity of your assumptions based on short-term performance ▪ Client is paralyzed because of short-term noise and refuses to do anything	▪ Reasons for original plan should be revisited and reviewed ▪ We are more concerned about where YOU are than where markets are! ▪ Place focus of discussion back on client's life needs rather than on performance ▪ Talk about how your approach incorporates risk management in its design
Self-Attribution *The "blame game" when things don't go well*	▪ Client blames you for all reversals but doesn't credit you for successes ▪ Client very aware of short-term wins and losses ▪ Client seeks out short-term trading opportunities	▪ Do not show concern over short-term fluctuations ▪ Do not take credit for positive short-term success ▪ Keep focus on role as primary advisor rather than as investment advisor
Ambiguity Aversion *"Paralysis by analysis"*	▪ Client allows bad news to affect decision-making ▪ Client focused on media commentary on economy or markets	▪ Use mental accounting to split up portfolio ▪ Focus client on how the component parts must all be invested in a different manner

Behavioral bias	Client behavior	Strategies to talk about 'risk'
Loss Aversion *"I want to take risks just as long as I can't lose any money"*	▪ Client focuses on paper losses continually ▪ Client expresses fear in initial discussion of plan ▪ Client refuses to buy into your advice if risk might be involved ▪ Client wishes to change plan at first sign of declining investment prices	▪ Focus client on parts of portfolio that are protected from loss ▪ Focus client on positives of investments such as dividend payment, low beta etc. (though never refer to it as 'beta'!) ▪ Discuss with client the short-term moves that the client might expect, and treat those as normal occurrences ▪ Help client understand difference between being a 'saver' and an 'investor'
Conservatism *"I can't afford to take losses at this stage of my life"*	▪ Client expresses concerns about risk in initial meeting or prior to implementation of strategy ▪ Client requires comfort that they would not be affected by market reversal	▪ Focus client on conservative elements (dividends, beta) of investment ▪ Help client understand that there is need for various kinds of assets in a conservative portfolio ▪ Reinforce benefit of professional management as part of risk management strategy

The Life-First Advisor ...

- Understands behavioral biases such as loss aversion
- Frames discussions so they focus on long-term goals, not short-term market moves
- Helps clients understand their own behavioral biases, so they can keep their eyes on the long term

18 | Social Bias

- **Eight 'compliance principles' guide human behavior**
- **Social influences tend to be ingrained and occur at the subconscious level**
- **The older a person is, the more ingrained these social factors become**

It's human nature for people to pay close attention to their place in their community. The need to interact in a social setting is innate and so strong that it can override even the most logical options in the decision-making process.

We've looked at the physiological, neural and psychological aspects of communicating with older people. We've also noted that emotion influences understanding and decision-making. The fourth influence on communications is social – or how older adults see themselves in relation to others.

While there's also an emotional element to the social influence on behavior, generally our social reactions are ingrained and often occur at the subconscious level. They are predispositions based on years of gauging our place in the world.

Social influence can be the main factor that contributes to crystallized thinking. We do things that fly in the face of reason because we need to 'fit in' or 'not stand out'. Psychologists call these behaviors 'compliance principles of human behavior' because they become unwritten rules that govern our behavior and describe how we're likely to act.

Eight principles can be at work in guiding how someone does something or makes a decision. Each of us is affected to some extent by all eight, though not always at the same magnitude.

The older a person is, the more ingrained these social factors become. This doesn't mean the desire to fit in, for example, increases with age. Most of us know older relatives or friends who actually become more rebellious as they age, simply because they get to a point in life where they don't feel they have anything to prove.

Principle 1 – Authority

We tend to listen to people whose credentials make them 'authorities'. Perceived expertise elicits respect and, ultimately, compliance.

If an advisor is seen to be an expert there's a better chance the client will listen to what they say and act on their advice. This is an area where your credentials reinforce your credibility.

Advisors often bring in outside experts to reinforce their advice, or use third-party research to add credibility. But be careful – the use of people who aren't really experts in their field can undermine your position and squander trust. This occurred back in the 1990s when advisors brought in high-profile speakers, advertising them as unbiased experts. Many advisors lost credibility when it turned out that some of these speakers were actually using them to sell products.

Some of the ways you can take advantage of the compliance principle of authority are:

- Know your products and services.
- Understand your client's life and business.
- Dress the way your client would like to see you.
- Acquire a problem-solving attitude, be goal oriented, focused and optimistic.
- Include your professional designation on your business card.

Establish yourself as an unquestioned expert in a subject so your clients would never question you. For example, you could position yourself as an expert in the seniors market, in a niche market such as a profession, demographic or gender, or as an advisor who focuses on a particular life stage, such as 'families in transition'.

Of course, you can always establish yourself as being an expert on your client …

Principle 2 – Reciprocity

We tend to want to do things for people who have done nice things for us.

For years, advisors have undertaken 'client appreciation' programs where they do something valuable for clients for no other motive than to show their appreciation for their business.

The principle of reciprocity is the foundation of your refer-ability. Clients will refer you to someone else if they feel you've done something of value for them. That's why we have trouble with the idea that you should always 'ask for the referral'. You shouldn't have to ask.

It's important to let clients know you'd be happy to work with others who might benefit from your expertise, but your clients have to feel you've done something special for them first.

That sense of 'special' might come from superior investment performance but also from a strong relationship that goes above and beyond meeting a client's basic needs.

Some of the ways you can respect the reciprocity effect are:

- Helping a client build a financial plan for the future that provides them with a sense of financial comfort now.

- Holding education events that help clients understand things important to them.

- Making them feel like you're a catalyst in their lives, by showing them how they can best use the financial resources they have.

Principle 3 – Rapport

People follow the advice of those they like. We like joining and belonging to groups and are inclined to favor members of, or contributors to, our 'gang'.

Your first goal in the client communications process is not be understood; it is to be liked. Clients want to be able to identify with those in whom they place their trust. They need to know you understand their unique needs as people and not just their financial issues.

We know many advisors have a hard time with this. They feel they're being 'unprofessional' simply by acting like a human being. "I'm not going to be friends with my clients", one advisor told us. "I'm their financial advisor and there's a wall that separates me from their personal life".

We wouldn't disagree – except your discussion with a client as a wealth advisor is very personal. No one is saying you should socialize with your clients, but you want them to feel your relationship with them is one of coach, educator or catalyst.

If your clients don't feel like there's an emotional connection they're less likely to refer you to someone else. After all, why would you want to refer someone you don't like to someone you do?

Advisors who want to leverage rapport as a way to build relationships and generate business should:

- Try to find ways to establish commonality, either in personal conversation or by becoming an expert in an area that's important to the client.

- Remember important personal information about your client to show them you care about them and not just their money.

- Meet clients at their home or place of business.

- Have client discussions around a table rather than over a desk.

Principle 4 – Reason

People have a natural tendency to respond positively to requests that make sense.

Let's reposition the idea of 'what makes sense': It's not what makes sense to you but what makes sense to the client.

When your clients decode your information, they're reframing it in terms they understand. In an earlier chapter we called this the 'hook' or the context and it's necessary if clients are to feel your information makes sense.

When you get them to 'teach back' information to you or get them to express an explicit need, you're confirming your information 'makes sense'.

Here are some tactics:

- Make sure you focus on the benefits of your solution to the client, rather than on the advantages the solution may have over a competitor's. After all, if the client doesn't need it, it really doesn't matter whether you are any better than your competition.

- Clearly communicate the benefits of your solutions in terms of a client's emotional needs.

- Get them to acknowledge a 'need' as part of your discovery conversation, to the point where they will articulate the words 'I need that', or 'We need to do this'.

Principle 5 – Efficiency

People tend to do things in the easiest way possible. They look for shortcuts, simple explanations, road maps or step-by-step processes.

It's natural not to want to do extra work unless you can see a direct benefit. When it comes to using our heads to process information, we are much more likely to respond to ideas presented in a way that makes it easy for us to see the connections.

Consider what happens when you present a difficult concept and your client isn't on the same page. This can occur when:

- You use your language and not theirs.
- They are in 'crystallized thinking' mode.
- You haven't sufficiently developed how your conversation relates to the specific needs they have.

You're expecting a client to 'connect the dots'. You believe that if they understand you they will benefit from your advice. Earlier, we called this the 'if I build it, they will come' approach, because it assumes all you have to do is speak and the world will listen!

Earlier, we talked about how the brain needs 'hooks' on which to hang new information. When you're catering to the principle of efficiency, you're telling your client's brain where to put the information and what to do with it.

Here are some strategies that will help you take advantage of the principle of efficiency:

- Use 'right-brain' pictures to illustrate a concept.
- Tie your conversation into a specific client need.
- Show the client the specific steps they can take to solve the problem.
- Make it easy for the client to make a decision and commitment by doing as much as possible for them.
- Distil your processes into easy-to-follow diagrams or flow charts.
- Anticipate client roadblocks or 'push-backs' and ensure you cover these first in any explanation you give. That helps ensure the client's thought process doesn't get interrupted.

Principle 6 – Consistency

People behave consistently with their previous behavior as well as with their self-concept.

In psychology, this is known as continuity theory. It reflects our need to fall back on the behaviors, ideals and perceptions we've held throughout our lives.

This subconscious driver or screen to our decision-making makes it more difficult for advisors to present new concepts that ask for a change in behavior. It doesn't mean we won't change, just that we need a very good reason to do so.

Generally, a client falls into 'crystallized thinking' mode when they have no desire to change how they view the information their advisor presents. It doesn't mean the information isn't valuable, just that the client's brain can't find the appropriate hook for it that will switch on fluid thinking.

Here are some ways you can work with the principle of consistency:

- Continually reinforce your value proposition with your clients so they'll remember what you actually do (and have the language to tell others).

- Always show the client how your solutions will improve on their present situation.

- Use an emotional appeal rather than a logical one, particularly for older clients who are even more likely to be locked into crystallized thinking.

Principle 7 – Social evidence

People tend to do what others (for whom they have respect) do.

You've seen this principle at work when you talk about 'keeping up with the Joneses'. You also use it every time you put a testimonial in a brochure or on your website.

Third-party endorsement is a powerful tool in convincing a client they should undertake a particular course of action. If you can show that someone with whom they identify has done the same thing successfully, they're much more likely to acquiesce.

We like success stories and the 'how-to' guides as to what made them work. We also to like underdog stories that show how someone can succeed against all odds. Such shows of determination give us confidence we can reach our goals too.

In your marketing material and conversations with clients, outline the types of clients you've worked with and how you've helped them. If you're going to target a market, include examples from that target group who have benefited from your advice.

Here are some other ways you can leverage the principle of social evidence:

- Join groups or associations in your target market to demonstrate a connection to your chosen group. This will give prospects in that group comfort you have some commonality and have been accepted by others.

- Hold client appreciation events so prospects and clients can see other clients who are happy with your relationship.

- Make good use of testimonials and stories that illustrate the benefits you have provided.

- Make sure your clients understand the recognition you have received in your industry through the designations you hold.

- Write articles as a subject matter expert to show clients and prospects you have respect in the community for your ideas.

Principle 8 – Scarcity

People tend to want something more if it is in short supply or time is running out.

Have you noticed how easy it is to sell something when you don't have much of it to sell? Those advisors who do a lot of new-issue business understand the power of scarcity in convincing someone they should invest.

The compliance principle at work here feeds off greed, but also off our desire for exclusivity. People like to feel they are part of an exclusive group with membership limited to a select few.

The relevance of 'social styles'

At a recent conference, we watched a psychologist discuss personality styles with a group of advisors. The goal of the presentation was to help them modify their style based on the social style of the client they were talking to.

One of the discussion topics was how to explain markets in a way that matches the client's personality. For example, participants were told a driver just wants the top-line facts, the analytical person wants the numbers, the expressive doesn't care and the amiable just wants a hug.

Advisors may believe they should discuss risk in a way that plays to their client's social style but we couldn't disagree more.

Regardless of how you perceive the social style of your client, you still have to understand what's going on emotionally when discussing both fear and greed. An analytical person still has an emotional response to risk, even if they're interested in your analysis of past performance.

Talking to your client about risk is as much about understanding what drives the client's fear as it is figuring out how to convey the information.

Your structure for discussing risk should be the same for all clients, regardless of their social style. Use your questions to gain a better understanding of the behavioral biases that are influencing their outlook and then employ a strategy based on the behavioral bias, not on the social style.

The limits of risk tolerance questionnaires

Many financial institutions use a form of risk tolerance questionnaire to identify and classify clients according to their capacity for risk. These questionnaires are also used to protect the advisor in the event a client comes back on them or the firm.

While there is some value to be gained from such an exercise, there are also potential limitations that may undermine its effectiveness. Here are some of the drawbacks:

Questionnaires may work well for institutions but not for individuals. Institutions can protect themselves legally by showing regulators they have done proper discovery. However, you won't uncover what's really behind the client's answers to the questions.

Behavioral biases need to be understood first. Clients will feed back answers based on what the question says. It's usually their 'fear center' that's answering the question rather than their logic. Since there are varying reasons why clients answer in the way they do, the advisor doesn't gain much insight into how to discuss the idea of 'risk' or the best strategy for moving the client forward.

Different risk tolerance questionnaires may yield different results. There are many different kinds of risk tolerance questionnaire. Some focus on a client's self-assessment while others present scenarios and then ask the client to react.

Many advisors and firms interpret the results too rigidly. Clients will only feed back what they know and may not be providing much insight into how they really feel about risk. Firms are stuck because they have to have a subjective measurement of a client's risk tolerance to protect themselves.

Risk tolerance assessment questionnaires are important, but they're only a start. In our view, they should be used in concert with behavioral assessment tools. Advisors should use their client interviews, especially Life-First Discovery, to gain greater insight into the client's real view on risk and then work with them to develop a strategy that gives them comfort.

The Life-First Advisor ...

- Understands the unwritten rules that govern our behavior
- Doesn't rely solely on risk tolerance questionnaires
- Understands what's really going on emotionally when they discuss risk and fear

19 | Designing a Better Business

In this book, we've focused primarily on your client value proposition. While most advisors focus 'below the line' (on investments and products), we've proposed repositioning this to 'above the line' (people, goals and objectives) in the form of life-based advice. That said, clearly there are other areas to consider in designing and building a world-class business.

The diagram below sets out in broad terms the six elements you should consider. Let's look at each of them in turn.

Designing a better business

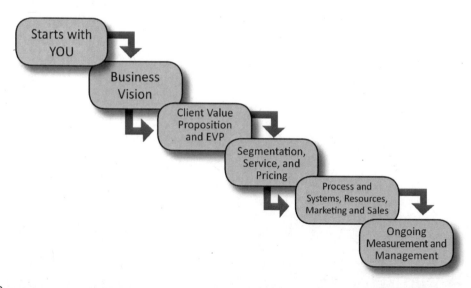

It starts with you

There are various stakeholders in an advice business and you are one of them. You have a life, goals and aspirations as well. We see some advisors want to grow and run increasingly large businesses, while others are quite happy to maintain a 'lifestyle' business. There's no right or wrong. But before you consider your business plan, ask yourself whether you have a personal plan. (For a template, email David at david@globaladviseralpha.com).

Business vision

It's an old saying but a good one: 'If you fail to plan, you plan to fail'. We continue to meet a surprising number of advisors without a documented business plan that they regularly review and update.

Have you considered a formal board or an advisory board structure? Have you considered current and future organizational charts, based on expected growth rates, to determine what your business might look like after one, three and five years? What roles need to be filled and when? Which tasks and roles are you currently undertaking? Which do you enjoy, and which could you delegate?

Client value proposition

So many clients receive suboptimal propositions. An even greater number of potential prospects choose not to seek advice at all. We strongly feel more people would seek out advice from client-centric, Life-First Advisors whose value proposition is focused 'above the line'.

In addition to what you've read in this book, you might also want to consider these areas:

- **Ideal client.** Have you defined clearly the sort of people you want to work with? Can you and your team articulate what that market looks like?

- **Niche markets**. Do you have a niche area of expertise you could focus on? Increased focus and efficiency leads to increased profitability.

- **Employee value proposition**. If you're moving from a practice to a business, you need to attract and retain good people. Why would someone want to work with you rather than the firm down the road? How would you articulate the attractions of your firm to prospective employees? (For a template, email David at david@globaladviseralpha.com).

Segmentation, service and pricing

Working on the interrelationships between client segments, client services and pricing is a continuum, a job that's never finished. This is a critical area you need to come back to each year as the market changes.

Typically, 80 percent of clients bring in about 20 percent of income. What's your breakdown and ratio? Without measuring these variables, your management, analysis and strategic decisions become much harder.

With precise client segmentation, you can release capacity and provide capital to meet your own goals. Remember, you're not only in the business of financial advice, you're in the business of getting paid for financial advice.

Processes and systems

Advisors frequently ask for help on workflow processes and the systems required to automate those processes. In undertaking these reviews, the key is being clear on your practice's end-to-end client experience. Reverse engineer the processes and document them. This needs to include, but is not limited to, all letters, emails, agendas, minutes and templates.

We often hear the term 'sales and marketing' but marketing needs to come before sales. What's your marketing plan to bring in an endless stream of pre-qualified referrals? Do you have a social media strategy?

For smaller businesses, do you have an external team that can assist you on matters you'd like to outsource? What areas will you in-source? What are you outsourcing? For example, in HR services do you have an employee manual, position descriptions, staff induction tools and documented KPIs that are SMART – specific, measurable, agreed, realistic, and time-based?

Measurement and management

"If you can't measure it, you can't manage it … ". What do you measure in your business? What would you like to know but don't measure? To name a few, there are share price, total revenue, ongoing revenue, EBIT or profit, and some key ratios such as revenue per full-time employee, revenue per advisor, and – typically driving the previous two – revenue per active client.

But we'll need to save some of that for our next book …

"It's not the unique things of a business that make it successful, it's the business's ability to do the ordinary things in an extraordinary way and to do those things consistently, predictably, effectively, day after day after day"

– Michael Gerber, The E Myth

Appendix 1:

40 Best Practices of the Life-First Advisor

Market positioning

1.   You position yourself as a primary advisor for clients, the one person who looks at the overall picture.
2.   You take a Life-First Approach to helping your clients, creating plans to meet their life needs, concerns, opportunities and goals.
3.   Your clients' 'wealth' is defined as their ability to do what they want, when they want and how they want. A 'wealth advisor' helps them get there.
4.   Your market positioning is 'above the line'. Your value to clients, prospects and centers of influence is in the clarity, insight and partnership you provide.
5.   You have identified a specific market niche that is your ideal client. You may have several niche markets where you have expertise.

Approach to investment management

1.   Your investment approach is strategic rather than tactical – you are more concerned about where your clients are in their lives than where the market is.
2.   You take a managed money approach, using the expertise of evidence-based professional managers to help your clients.
3.   You pay close attention to fees and tax issues.
4.   You take a diversified, evidence-based approach to positioning client portfolios, drawing on sound investment theory and practice to managing their nest eggs.
5.   You help clients maintain discipline by understanding short-term 'noise' issues that must be 'managed through' to mitigate worry or concern on a day-to-day basis.

Client education

1. Your clients can articulate your approach to wealth management and you have educated them in the language they can use to tell someone else.

2. You run regular client education programs, focusing on topics that fit into the life issues they face and calling on outside experts to augment your presentations.

3. Your clients view you as a 'catalyst' in providing them with the information they need to think about their money and their life through your seminars, workshops, newsletters etc.

4. You understand the principles of behavioral finance and help your clients understand how their behavior can affect their futures.

5. You are continually looking for client-specific education pieces appropriate for each client's unique situation.

Approach to creating a financial plan

1. The foundation of your financial planning approach is to understand your clients' needs, concerns, opportunities and goals in key areas of their lives.

2. The solutions you present focus on solving life issues and tend to be multi-faceted rather than settling on a single need or product.

3. You follow the six-step CFP planning process and your clients are aware of your disciplined and structured approach. Life-first lets you understand even more detail to your process.

4. You are proactive in your planning, using meetings and contacts to keep the client focused on life issues and the need to plan for them financially.

5. You plan for life transitions, identifying areas that need to be planned for to help clients make the transitions as easily as possible.

Discovery process

1.   You have a clearly articulated discovery process that your clients can understand and articulate to someone else.
2.   Your Life-First Discovery process focuses first on understanding life issues, needs and concerns before assessing the financial implications.
3.   Your process is visual and engages the client emotionally in the process.
4.   You practice the skills of the empathic listener and develop your conversational skills.
5.   You tie the solutions you present to the life issues you uncovered in the discovery process.

Leveraging your team

1.   You have professional contacts in all life areas, financial planning and investment management areas to support you and your clients in areas where you require additional expertise.
2.   You make use of your team members to so you can spend more time with your clients.
3.   All of your team understand your value proposition and reinforce it with clients, prospects and centers of influence.
4.   All of your team have clearly defined responsibilities and are comfortable in their roles.
5.   Your external 'team of experts' is part of your team and you take on the role of team leader.

Client contact

1.   You have a systematic and disciplined approach to client contact based on client need and segmentation.
2.   On at least a monthly basis you make use of various client contact strategies to keep yourself 'top of mind'.
3.   You insist on regular face-to-face meetings with your top clients where possible (at least twice a year and more if needed).
4.   Your clients must have a positive emotional connection with you.
5.   You make use of social media where practical to maintain contact with your clients.

Running your business

1.   You have a well-defined business plan that treats your practice as a business. Business development is integral, as is a defined strategy for prospecting, target marketing and working through centers of influence. You also have a clear picture of revenue and expenses.

2.   You understand that to be successful in your practice you must combine technical expertise, entrepreneurship and business management skills. You are aware of your strengths and weaknesses and use team members to support you in those areas that are not your strong points.

3.   You have learned to leverage your time by making use of outside resources such as TAMPS (Turnkey Asset Management Providers), consultants and advisory board members, as well as internal resources.

4.   You believe in continuing education for yourself and your team.

5.   You seek work/life balance and encourage it in your team so you are able to enjoy what you do and give your clients the full benefit of your attention.

Appendix 2:

Answering the 'real' question

In Chapter 8 we looked at the 'iceberg metaphor'. We talked about identifying the real question behind the nominal one, and how 'deep' you did or didn't need to go in responding. Here are some other questions you might face and how to address them at differing depths:

Question a client might ask	What's the underlying question?	Level 1 Here's 'what' we do to protect you
Can you explain what a wealth advisor does and why I should do business with you? Why should I choose your firm over someone else?	*I haven't had a great experience in the past and I didn't see any value in the advisors I've worked with. All firms seem like they do the same thing and they all market the same way. What is it that you do that's any different?*	We take a unique approach to working with you, to investing your money and to providing you with financial planning guidance. We only work with a select group of clients who would benefit from the advice we provide. Other advisors manage money. Our firm focuses on relationships by first understanding the things in life that are important to clients. Only then do we create strategies that fit their unique needs. Our interests are aligned with our clients, so we don't make recommendations we wouldn't use ourselves in the same circumstances.
Shouldn't I wait for more certainty in the markets before I commit more money to my investment portfolio?	*I don't really understand how investing and investment markets work. Do I have a big risk of losing my money? Isn't market timing the best way to succeed in the market? Shouldn't you invest when things are good?*	If you take a long-term perspective, short-term market moves aren't as important. We successfully manage money through all kinds of market conditions because of the approach we take. It's important to recognize that you invest to reach your life goals and address your needs, opportunities and concerns. Investing is about you – not about where markets are.

Level 2 And here's 'how' we do it	Level 3 Here's the detail
We use an academic and science-based approach to designing solutions and strategies. We use our extensive education and experience to help you while also accessing our team of experts to provide additional support. We have an ongoing partnership with our clients through the ages and stages of their lives.	Independence & fiduciary standard Suitability standard, 12b-1 fees, brokerage firm scandals, Principles: discipline, cost minimization, controlled risk taking, tax considerations, Credentials, planning and investment tools. Alignment with world-class strategic partners.
We take a passive vs active approach. This is an evidence-based approach with an academic foundation Our process is goal-driven and proactive rather than reactive. We focus on controllable factors. We focus on what works, versus what 'sells'.	Principles: discipline, cost minimization, controlled risk taking, tax considerations, etc. Investment management experience, process and tools. Suitability standard, 12b-1 fees, brokerage firm scandals, etc. Structure determines performance. Diversification is essential.

Question a client might ask	What's the underlying question?	Level 1 Here's 'what' we do to protect you
Isn't there too much risk in the stock market for me to expose my retirement portfolio?	*This isn't play money – it's my retirement nest egg. I can't afford to lose any of it because I can't make it back. What if the world 'melts down'?*	We take a conservative approach to investment management based on our academic understanding of how markets work. Your retirement portfolio was set up to meet your retirement goals. We continue to monitor your portfolio to ensure we stay on track and we will make changes if we believe it is in your best interests. We firmly believe in the concept of asset allocation to protect you from the short-term ups and downs of the market.
Why should I pay fees to a wealth advisor? Can't I do this myself?	*I don't understand what you do and I've never really seen the value of paying an advisor for bad advice. If I must have an advisor, then make it an advisor who doesn't charge much.*	We provide you with our experience, expertise and guidance to help you reach your goals. Our role is not to do things for you that you could do for yourself. Rather, we are like your Chief Financial Officer. We help you clarify your goals, concerns, opportunities and needs. Only then can we build the right strategy for you. We work with you on an ongoing basis to ensure your plan is always on track to reach your goals. Our service is focused more on where you are in your life than where the markets are on a day-to-day basis.
I really like your philosophy and firm but I have a long-term relationship with my current advisor and I know you emphasize relationships. Therefore, I'm not ready to make a move at this time.	*I don't see the need to change though there was something about your value proposition that I really liked. Is there anything I'm missing about why I should think about changing?*	We're not setting out to take away the relationship you have with your current advisor but to start a new one with us. Many of our clients find a second opinion beneficial when it comes to reaching longer-term goals. Our approach to wealth management is unique and we often work with clients who also have other advisors specializing in other areas but who do not provide the overall service we provide.

Level 2 And here's 'how' we do it	Level 3 Here's the detail
We take a passive vs active approach. This is an evidence-based approach with an academic foundation Our process is goal-driven and proactive rather than reactive. We focus on controllable factors. We focus on what works, versus what 'sells'.	Principles: discipline, cost minimization, controlled risk taking, tax considerations, etc. Investment management experience, process and tools. Suitability standard, 12b-1 fees, brokerage firm scandals, etc. Structure determines performance, Diversification is essential.
We have an ongoing process from discovery through strategy, implementation and review. We help our clients meet their important needs: • Enjoying and protecting lifestyle • Helping and protecting family • Planning ahead for the expected and unexpected • Creating a sense of financial comfort • Building a legacy. The personal relationships we create with our clients help them through the ages and stages of their lives.	Education, certification and designations. Various services and support we provide for clients. Methodology for managing money. Team of experts to support clients. Quality and size of firm. Reputation and longevity as wealth advisors.
We can be your 'primary advisor'. Our focus is on wealth management, goal setting and comprehensive planning, not just investment management. We can add to the relationships you already have.	Company and practice services. Testimonials from clients who also have other advisors. Description of what we do that might be different from other advisors. Overview of the strength of the firm

Question a client might ask	What's the underlying question?	Level 1 Here's 'what' we do to protect you
Why would I buy fixed income in a low interest rate environment? Why should I pay a fee to ladder low yielding CDs when I could buy CDs at an equivalent yield from a few local banks?	*I think all fixed income is bad right now and I can't see the investment value. I think we are going to be in a low interest rate environment for some time. I also don't like paying fees because I don't see the value and trying to sell me fixed income is a typical example of paying something for nothing .*	We take a systematic, academically rigorous approach to managing your money. One of the foundations of our successful approach is our belief that asset allocation is key to long-term performance. Regardless of where interest rates are, we recommend clients maintain a fixed-income allocation to reduce the volatility in their portfolio. It's always difficult to predict the short-term moves in any market. For that reason, we like to manage the interest rate risk by laddering your fixed-income portfolio so we maintain flexibility. The value we provide as your portfolio manager is to take a longer-term view of your investments and make sure we match them against the goals you have set. You pay us to use our best knowledge and understanding to ignore the short term and focus on an approach that works in all kinds of markets.
Why should I pay fees when my account loses its value?	*I don't see the value in the fees I pay, particularly when I don't get performance.*	Our measure of performance is whether we are able to reach the goals you set for your investments at the outset. You don't pay us to outguess markets in the short term and we can't deliver on that. Our job is to develop the right longer-term strategies for you, strategies that don't depend on short-term moves in the market. We continually monitor your portfolio performance and will make changes that may need to be made as your circumstances change.

Level 2 And here's 'how' we do it	Level 3 Here's the detail
This is how our asset allocation works. We focus on predictability of investment return. This is how layering maintains portfolio flexibility and reduces risk.	Correlation between asset classes. Efficient frontier. Historical real returns. Return illustrations.
Let's look again your long-term goals, risk tolerance and strategic approach. Our investment management methodology focuses on the long term, positioning client for the future There are long-term risks in short-term thinking.	Historic market information. Rebound of bear market illustration Structure determines long-term performance. Passive vs active

Question a client might ask	What's the underlying question?	Level 1 Here's 'what' we do to protect you
Why didn't you do something to prevent my account from decreasing so much in the market meltdown? Does 'buy and hold' really work?	*You should have been able to forecast which way the market was going. There must have been something you could have done. You didn't adjust your overall strategy in the wake of turbulent markets. I'm worried I may lose my nest egg because you can't react to short-term market moves.*	Short-term market movements are difficult to predict, so we constructed a portfolio that has the best chance of reaching the goals you set. We continually review the situation to identify opportunities and threats to these long-term goals. If your investment goals change, we can review our approach and ensure we are still able to use our expertise to help you reach long-term goals rather than short-term trading success.
How are my assets protected?	*I'm worried I might lose my money if anything happens to your company. I fear the unknown because we are in volatile times. This is my nest egg and I can't afford to lose it.*	All of your money is held in a trust account that is separate from our practice. We do not hold your assets as part of our practice. Our rigorous internal compliance provides an additional layer of protection by ensuring that rules and regulations are always followed. We provide you with a continuous reporting process to help you keep track of your investments and their value.

Level 2 And here's 'how' we do it	Level 3 Here's the detail
Let's look again at your long-term goals, risk tolerance and strategic approach. Our investment management methodology focuses on the long term, positioning client for the future There are long-term risks in short-term thinking.	Performance of markets over time Rebound of bear market illustration Individual company price illustrations over time Structure determines performance Passive investing vs. active investing
We use an independent third party custodian. The system has checks and balances – regulator and investment fund safeguards, plus our own processes, are all designed to protect your money. We make it convenient for you to stay on top of your financial situation through online access to your account, regular updates and new information that may affect you.	SIPC, E&O insurance, etc. Publicly traded securities. Regulations & governance.

Appendix 3:

Retirement Vision Worksheet

In Chapter 14 we looked at the Life-First Advisor's role as someone who can help clients clarify what they *really* want their retirement to look like. This worksheet provides a guide for discussion. Don't give it to the client to fill out but work through it with them, making notes as they talk.

Your Retirement Vision

Let's take a quick inventory of your retirement vision today

1. In what year do you believe that your present work situation will change?

_____

2. Choose the terms that will best describe this next phase:

- ○ Not working at anything
- ○ Working part-time at the same job
- ○ Working part-time at a new job
- ○ Starting a new career
- ○ Becoming self-employed
- ○ Consulting in my area of expertise
- ○ Developing a second business
- ○ Buying a new business
- ○ Continuing to work full-time by choice
- ○ Perpetual leisure/relaxation
- ○ Building or renewing social relationships

○ Spending more time with family, friends

○ Doing what I want, when I want

○ Focusing on hobbies

○ Travelling more than three months a year

○ Education or study

○ Learn new skills

○ Volunteering or community involvement

○ Developing talents

○ Moving to a new location

○ Addressing health or fitness issues

○ Becoming more "spiritual"

○ Managing my investments

○ Doing what I do now

3. At this time, the idea of retirement makes me feel:

1	2	3	4	5	6	7	8	9	10
Sad			Neither Good nor Bad						Excited

4. At this moment in your life, how would you describe your retirement planning program?

○ Well thought out

○ Just a financial plan

○ Have had some thoughts about it

○ Haven't thought about it

○ Don't intend to retire

5. What are your greatest concerns about the future?

- ○ Not having enough assets or income
- ○ Inflation
- ○ Lengthy illness
- ○ Difficult family relationships
- ○ Moving to a new area and then not liking it
- ○ Moving to a new home and then not liking it
- ○ Being bored
- ○ Not being productive or useful
- ○ Missing friends from my work life
- ○ Investment crisis
- ○ Other _____

6. When I retire...

Complete the following sentences as many times as you can. When you think you've run out of ideas, wait at least two minutes to see if more ideas come.

When I retire, I will...	When I retire, I will feel...	When I retire, I want to...

Barry LaValley

Barry LaValley is Principal, Right-Brain Advisor and is a leading authority in the North American Financial Services industry on client communication and financial gerontology. His work has taken him around the world, including presentations in Great Britain, Europe, Australia, New Zealand, Mainland China, the US and Canada. In addition, he coaches advisors across the Globe on the "Right-brain Approach" to client communication and how clients think, act and make decisions.

Barry started his career as a retail advisor in Canada in 1980 after graduating from University in the seventies. He moved to the Mutual Funds industry in 1987 as a Senior sales executive and finished that stage of his career with Fidelity in 1997.

Since that time, Barry LaValley focus has been on two areas: first, the issue of client communications and the psychology behind how advisors can "make their message stick". Second, he has been actively involved in research and education on Retirement transition through his company The Retirement Lifestyle Center. He conducts retirement sessions for both advisors and clients across the Globe.

Barry is one of the founders of the "life planning approach to financial planning" and was a contributor to the seminal meeting on financial life planning in St. Louis in 2002. In the past two decades, he has championed what he calls the "Life-first approach" which outlines how advisors can tie financial issues to life needs, concerns and goals.

Barry LaValley is an active writer and educator. He was a contributor (along with Carol Anderson) to Mitch Anthony's book "Your Clients for Life" in 2003. He expanded on his ideas in 2005 in the book "Put the Life into your Practice" and has recently released "The Retirement Advisor" and "The Life-First Advisor" in 2017.

Barry and his wife Melissa live in Nanaimo, B.C. Canada

David Haintz

David is a CFP and a past director of the
Financial Planning Association of Australia
(FPA), in which time he was instrumental
in the push for professionalism. He has
had a 28 year career with his own firm,
and subsequently became a founding
director of Shadforth Financial Group
(in a 13 way script for script roll up - at
the time $80m revenue and $25m ebit),
with over 100 advisers; which listed on
the ASX and was taken over in 2014 for
$670m - at the time $13b FUM, $165m
revenue, and $58m EBIT.

David was the sixth adviser in Australia to be awarded a Fellow of the FPA,
and served on the FPA Disciplinary Committee for seven years, the FPA
Professionalism Committee for six years, and was a National Judge at the
FPA's inaugural Value of Advice Awards. He is a founding trustee of the
Future2 Foundation, and lectured at the FINSIA for six years, and current sits
on the international Financial Planning Standards Board – Developing Markets
Practice Management Working Group.

He has presented at international conventions such as the UK Institute of
Financial Planning, and the South African Institute of Financial Planning
conferences; in 2016 had consulting engagements in 18 countries including
diverse locations such as India and Germany.

David remains the only adviser in Australia to be awarded the two prominent
awards - Australian Financial Planner of the Year (2005), and Australian Best
Practice of the Year (2004).

Whilst at Shadforth, he originated and on-boarded more new clients, more
FUM, and more revenue than any other of the 120 advisers, each and every
year, of the 4 years he advised post-merger, before moving into a advice
leadership and coaching role in 2012, where he was able to implement
a program that took national client conversions from 25% to 67% in 12
months, on double the average FUM rate of the previous 4 years.

Having departed Shadforth in 2015, he has established Global Adviser
Alpha – a B2B consultancy helping leading global advice businesses
become world class and achieve outstanding result for all stakeholders.

Testimonials

We both have been fortunate to work around the world with advisors and their firms. As part of the process of writing our book we have provided advance copies to some of the well-respected experts in our industry.

From the US

"Barry LaValley and David Haintz deliver a wealth of insight about the changing landscape of the financial advisory business. By sizing up the complex role of the advisor, they offer a new model for success based on a deep understanding of where clients are and, more importantly, where clients aspire to be."
Dave Butler, Co-CEO and Head of Global Financial Advisor Services, Dimensional Fund Advisors
Austin, Texas, United States

"Real financial advice is all about that messy overlap of money and meaning. Of course the problem with that reality is that very few advisors have been taught exactly how to navigate that landscape. What David and Barry have provided here is not really a book...it's a map! Follow it with care."
Carl Richards
Behavior Gap, Author and New York Times Columnist
Park City Utah, United States

"There are very few people in the world who understand Financial Advisors and great advice as well as Barry and David. Their lifetimes of learning are now documented to help others provide the care to the folks who need it most. This is a must read for those who simply want to improve their care to clients."
Alex Potts
CEO, Loring Ward Incorporated
San Jose CA, United States

"In this book Barry LaValley and David Haintz provide important insights that form the foundations of building and growing meaningful client relationships. This work is relevant and easily applicable to everyday practice. Barry and David are masters at providing essential information and this book is an essential guide to any financial professional who wants to be an elite wealth advisor. Barry LaValley has been bringing the critical lessons of brain science to the wealth advisor community for years. Nobody does it better."

Mont Levy
Principal, Buckingham Asset Management
St. Louis, MO, United States

From Australia

"The financial services industry is about to be disrupted and not before time! For too long the industry has served the money first, not the client. To survive this momentous change, financial advisors will need to place the client at the centre of everything they do, and the 'Life First Advisor' will help them do just that. It is a must read for any financial advisor wanting to grow and prosper."

David Andrew
Founder and CEO, Capital Partners Private Wealth
Perth, Australia

"David Haintz and Barry LaValley have hit the nail on the head! They know 'why' they do what they do and they recognise 'why' advisers are going to have to help people know 'why' they are taking control of their destiny. Each of us have a unique purpose in life. We want to work with people who will enable us to unlock the potential we have within us with our talents and resources that can be put to use to achieve our objective in life. Financial mastery is one of the keys to maximising our potential. The advice business has to adapt to become an enabler and not merely a distributor. People don't buy what we do, they buy why we do it and this book helps us to clarify that 'why'."

Kevin Bailey
Founding Director of Shadforth Financial Group, and former FPA Director
Melbourne, Australia

"David Haintz is passionate about our profession and the positive difference we make in the lives of our clients. It is wonderful that he has distilled his wealth of experience into this book. At the end of the day it is all about the client story that sits behind the numbers."
Matthew Rowe
Former Chairman of the FPA
Adelaide, Australia

"Drawing on decades of experience, David and Barry reset the focus for good advice to clients' own lives. This is not only a refreshing and principled approach, it's a successful one."
Jim Parker, writer and communications professional
Sydney, Australia

"This book contains an invaluable set of tools for the adviser who really wants to put clients first and learn from genuine experts. The breadth of insights and learning included is so far reaching; whether it be brain science from physiology to psychology or the understanding of human behaviour as it relates to money or the more practical "how to do it stuff" of advice process, client communication, marketing, contact strategies or the 40 Best Practices ..this is a great book, congratulations Barry and David"
Peter Mancell
Chairman, Global Association of Independent Advisors
Burnie, Tasmania, Australia

From the U.K.

"All around the world, we're seeing a great awakening in the financial advice profession. For too long it's been far too focused on products. But picking products is not how advisers add value -- it never was -- and increasingly the emphasis is on areas where a good adviser really does make a difference. First and foremost, advice is about the client, and helping them do the things they want to do while they have the opportunity. This book is for advisers who want to do the right thing -- and build a world class business in the process. It's long overdue."
Robin Powell
Author and Principal, The Evidence-based Investor
Birmingham, UK

"The Life-First Advisor is an essential read for all financial advisors and planners. Financial Life Planners will read this with a degree of recognition and comfort that they adopt this way of working. Those who still focus simply on the money part will shudder to their core, and start to reflect on the way in which they operate their businesses in the future. From explaining why the life-first approach is so relevant for clients and advisers alike, right through to designing a practice to enable the work to happen naturally, this is a step by step guide on future-proofing your business. For any new advisers starting out, you would do well to read this, and model your business accordingly. Without doubt, a blue-print for any practice who wants to put their clients' Life-First."
Jeremy Squibb DipPFS, RLP
Financial Life Planner & Head of Life Planning
Serenity Financial Planning
London, England

From Canada

"Barry LaValley & David Haintz help advisors dig beneath the surface to uncover what's truly important to clients. Living a life with purpose is the ultimate goal, but how do you get there? How do you increase the value you offer clients and make a meaningful impact while competing against regulatory and technology threats to your business? Read on to find out and become an enlightened advisor that not only survives, but thrives in the future."
Sybil Verch
SVP, National Director Wealth Management, Raymond James Ltd.,
Private Client Group, Victoria, B.C. Canada

"The way in which advisors add value to the lives of their clients has changed. Knowing that is one thing; doing something about it is a very different challenge. In this evidence-based book, Barry LaValley and David Haintz give you the tools to take stock and take action. Their concept of 'life-first planning' gets to the heart and future of the advisory relationship."
Julie Littlechild
Founder, AbsoluteEngagement.com
Toronto, Ontario, Canada

"Digitalization of the advisor's traditional value proposition of financial and investment planning and money management is commoditizing the delivery of advice. How then, are advisors to demonstrate value to their clients? The answer, I believe, rests in their ability to take on a new role that cannot be assumed by technology — the role of counsellor, coach, confidante. Regrettably, many advisors are unprepared for that upgrade and there are few resources to educate and equip them for their new responsibilities — until now. The Life-First Advisor is the first and only fully comprehensive guide I have seen that not only establishes the required new principles of client engagement, but is also replete with checklists, processes, scripts and advice — all designed to enable advisors of today to become the advisors of tomorrow. If that is your ambition, this book is a great place to start!"

George Hartman
Author, President, Market Logics Inc
Toronto, Ontario, Canada

"Most in the industry can see a change coming in the way that advice is delivered and the role that the advisor will play in a client's life. This book by Barry and David is a great roadmap for how advisors can prepare their practice for change. It is a step-by-step instruction for a communications and financial planning strategy that will not only set the advisor apart but form the foundation of what future advisors will be doing."

Wade Baldwin
Chair- Advocis, The Financial Advisors Association of Canada
Calgary, Alberta, Canada

From Singapore

"This is a beautiful and practical book on advising financial matters and managing client relationships. It aims to offer a holistic approach to suit the needs of the ever-changing clients. A good read, indeed."

Kimmis Pun
Managing Director - Private Banking
Singapore

From New Zealand

"David Haintz is without question a thought leader within Australasian financial planning. His expertise has been honed over many years as a successful private client adviser, businessman and business mentor. I've known David for a long time and have often enjoyed seeing first-hand the positive impact he has on clients and advisers. David is a natural teacher and excels at educating investors to make smarter choices and survive the vagaries of the market. David <u>always</u> makes a real difference. This beautifully written book nails an advisers true value proposition, which is to align investors' money with their goals and values. In short, it should be the gold standard template for advisers and investors alike."

Scott Alman
Managing Director, Consilium
Christchurch, New Zealand

From Malaysia

"Right off, I can see that the content of this book is very relevant to the profession especially in raising the bar. I note that Barry, in his acknowledgement, had penned "While I don't feel that advisors are life-planners, I do think that their clients need to be when they develop a long-term plan." I feel another book on financial planning is waiting in the wings as this one takes off first. I congratulate both Barry and David for putting their hearts and souls into sharing their wealth of experiences in this book. Wishing the both of you every success in your book launch."

Linnet Lee CFP
Chief Executive Officer, Financial Planning Association of Malaysia
Kuala Lumpur, Malaysia

From India

"Human mind has embedded conditioning of centuries to stay in a constant state of conflict and we run a genuine risk of computers taking over basic functions of the human mind. Noted Indian philosopher, J. Krishnamurty had predicted this decades ago. Robo- Advisory is here to take over all logic based functions of the Financial Advisor. To survive and grow in this disruptive world of Money, we need to completely re- frame our relationship with our clients. 'The Life-First Advisor' is a marvellous tool kit to lead to us to this remarkable journey of transformation of our mind as a Financial Advisor and an Investor. Having known David for decades, this book is another piece of excellence which comes from a lifetime of learning of intricacies of client behaviour. Well done Barry and David. This book transcends boundaries of culture and is relevant to an Advisor or an Investor anywhere in the world."
Rajiv Bajaj
Chairman, Bajaj Capital
New Delhi, India

From Uganda

"Reading through Life-First Advisor, I got a rude awakening! Times are changing and so are my clients. If I continue serving my clients the "same" menu that worked so well in the past, as a Retirement specialist, I may well become irrelevant. A good read for anyone in estate, financial and retirement planning. The book is truly a breath of fresh air in this rapidly changing field."
Petero Wamala, MA.
Retirement specialist. NLP master practitioner. Author and speaker.
Kampala, Uganda